# Building Dynamic Websites with PHP and MySQL

## Learn Server-Side Programming with a Focus on Security and Scalability

Greyson Chesterfield

# Contents

Introduction ........................................................................7

What is a Dynamic Website? ......................................................8

Importance of Server-Side Programming .................................11

The Role of PHP and MySQL in Building Dynamic Websites..............12

Overview of the Book's Structure ...............................................14

Setting Expectations for Security and Scalability.......................15

Chapter 1: Introduction to PHP and MySQL .............................18

What is PHP? ..........................................................................18

What is MySQL? ......................................................................21

Setting Up a Development Environment ....................................23

Your First PHP Script...............................................................25

Chapter 2: Understanding the Basics of Server-Side
Programming ....................................................................28

What is Server-Side Programming? ...........................................28

How PHP Works on the Server .................................................31

Difference Between Client-Side and Server-Side Code.........................33

How PHP Handles HTTP Requests .............................................34

The Role of Forms and User Input.............................................36

Chapter 3: Introduction to Databases .........................................39

What is a Database? .................................................................39

Introduction to Relational Databases ........................................40

Overview of SQL (Structured Query Language)...........................42

Creating a Database with MySQL ..............................................44

Simple SQL Queries (CREATE, SELECT, INSERT) ..........................45

Working with Tables in MySQL .................................................48

Real-World Examples of Tables for a Blog or E-Commerce Site .........49

Chapter 4: Connecting PHP to MySQL ......................................51

How PHP Connects to MySQL....................................................51

Introduction to the MySQLi and PDO Extensions in PHP ..................53

Writing Simple PHP Scripts to Connect to a Database.........................57

Displaying Data Dynamically on a Webpage .................................62

Chapter 5: Creating and Managing Forms in PHP.....................66

HTML Forms and PHP.............................................................66

Handling User Input in PHP.....................................................68

Validating User Input.............................................................71

Form Handling and Storing Data in MySQL ..............................75

Chapter 6: Working with Sessions and Cookies .......................79

What are Sessions? .................................................................79

Real-World Example: User Login Session .................................80

What are Cookies?.................................................................84

Securing Sessions and Cookies ...............................................87

Chapter 7: Implementing User Authentication and Authorization
.........................................................................................90

Building a Secure Login System ...............................................90

User Roles and Permissions ....................................................95

Securing User Authentication and Authorization .......................99

Chapter 8: Interacting with Dynamic Content........................102

CRUD Operations (Create, Read, Update, Delete).....................102

Displaying Dynamic Content with PHP....................................112

Chapter 9: Introduction to Object-Oriented PHP ....................117

What is Object-Oriented Programming (OOP)?.........................117

Explaining OOP Concepts .....................................................118

How OOP Makes PHP More Scalable and Maintainable...............122

Creating a Simple PHP Class..................................................123

OOP Principles in Practice: Real-World Example of User Management
.........................................................................................126

Chapter 10: Advanced MySQL Queries..................................130

Complex SQL Queries...........................................................130

Real-World Examples: Creating Reports and Querying Data from
Multiple Tables ...................................................................135

Optimizing SQL Queries.................................................................137

Chapter 11: Security Best Practices in PHP and MySQL.........141

Common Security Risks in Web Development......................................141

Securing PHP Code...............................................................................146

Securing MySQL Databases..................................................................149

Chapter 12: Building a Simple Content Management System
(CMS)...................................................................................................152

What is a CMS?.......................................................................................152

The Need for Dynamic, Editable Websites..........................................154

Overview of a Simple CMS with PHP and MySQL.............................155

Key Features of a CMS...........................................................................157

Real-World Example of Building a Basic CMS for a Blog..................160

Chapter 13: Introduction to MVC (Model-View-Controller)
Architecture........................................................................................165

What is MVC?..........................................................................................166

Explanation of the MVC Design Pattern.............................................167

How MVC Separates Concerns in PHP Applications..........................169

Building an MVC Application with PHP...............................................170

Chapter 14: File Uploads and Handling Media.......................177

Uploading Files with PHP.....................................................................177

Storing and Displaying Media..............................................................182

Best Practices for Managing Media Files.............................................186

Chapter 15: Handling Large-Scale Data and Optimizing
Performance........................................................................................188

Scalability Challenges in Web Development........................................188

What Makes a Website Scalable?..........................................................189

Optimizing PHP for Performance.........................................................193

Scaling MySQL Databases.....................................................................195

Chapter 16: Using PHP Frameworks (Laravel, Symfony).......199

Why Use a PHP Framework?.................................................................199

Introduction to Laravel.........................................................................201

**Symfony Overview** ................................................................205

Chapter 17: Testing and Debugging PHP Applications ...........209

**Importance of Testing in Web Development** ........................................209

**Debugging Techniques in PHP** .............................................................211

**Unit Testing and Test-Driven Development (TDD)** ..............................214

Chapter 18: Deploying Your PHP and MySQL Website ........219

**Preparing for Production** .......................................................................219

**Deploying on Shared Hosting, VPS, and Cloud Platforms** ................222

**Maintenance and Updates** ....................................................................226

Conclusion: Next Steps for Mastery in Building Dynamic
Websites with PHP and MySQL ...........................................229

**Next Steps for Mastery** ........................................................................229

**Recommended Resources for Continued Learning** ...........................232

**Encouragement to Keep Practicing with Real-World Projects** ...........234

**Building and Growing Real-World Projects** .........................................236

Appendix: Glossary of Terms and Resources for Further
Learning.................................................................................239

**Glossary of Terms** ................................................................................239

**Resources for Further Learning** ..........................................................244

# COPYRIGHT

# DISCLAIMER

The information provided in this book is for general informational purposes only. All content in this book reflects the author's views and is based on their research, knowledge, and experiences. The author and publisher make no representations or warranties of any kind concerning the completeness, accuracy, reliability, suitability, or availability of the information contained herein.

This book is not intended to be a substitute for professional advice, diagnosis, or treatment. Readers should seek professional advice for any specific concerns or conditions. The author and publisher disclaim any liability or responsibility for any direct, indirect, incidental, or consequential loss or damage arising from the use of the information contained in this book.

# Introduction

In today's digital landscape, building dynamic, interactive websites has become an essential skill for developers. As businesses and users increasingly rely on online platforms for communication, commerce, and entertainment, the demand for websites that can handle complex interactions and provide real-time updates has grown significantly. Dynamic websites, powered by server-side programming languages and databases, are at the heart of this transformation.

This book is designed to guide you through the process of building dynamic websites using PHP and MySQL, two of the most popular technologies in web development. By focusing on practical, real-world examples, we will explore the essentials of server-side programming, database management, and how to create secure and scalable applications that can grow with the demands of your users.

In this chapter, we'll start by understanding the key differences between static and dynamic websites. We'll also introduce PHP and MySQL, two powerful tools used to create dynamic content. Finally, we'll set the stage for the rest of the book by outlining the goals and expectations you should have for learning these technologies.

# What is a Dynamic Website?

To understand what a dynamic website is, it's important first to understand the difference between static and dynamic websites.

## Static Websites

A static website is essentially a collection of files, typically HTML files, that are served to the user exactly as they are stored on the server. Each time a user accesses the page, the same content is delivered. Static websites are relatively simple to build and don't require server-side processing. They are best suited for informational websites or portfolios where content doesn't change frequently.

- **Characteristics of Static Websites**:
    - Content is fixed and doesn't change unless manually updated.
    - Every user sees the same content.
    - Limited interactivity and functionality.

## Dynamic Websites

Dynamic websites, on the other hand, are more sophisticated. They are capable of generating content on the fly, typically in response to user input or real-time data from a database. Unlike static websites, dynamic websites can provide personalized experiences for each visitor by retrieving and displaying data from a server, processing user input, and interacting with databases to update content.

A dynamic website is usually powered by server-side programming languages like PHP, Python, or Ruby, which process requests, interact with databases, and generate HTML content on the fly. PHP, in particular, is a popular server-side language that is widely used for building dynamic websites.

- **Characteristics of Dynamic Websites**:
    - Content is generated in real-time based on user interactions or data.
    - Allows for interactive features such as forms, user accounts, and real-time updates.
    - Can display personalized content to each user.

**Examples of Dynamic Websites**

Dynamic websites are all around us. Some of the most common examples include:

- **Social Media Platforms**: Websites like Facebook, Twitter, and Instagram are dynamic because they deliver personalized content based on user activity, preferences, and interactions. When you log in, you see content that is tailored to you, such as friend suggestions, posts, and advertisements.

- **E-Commerce Sites**: Online shopping websites like Amazon or eBay are dynamic because they interact with databases to provide real-time product listings, prices, and availability. The content changes depending on what products a user searches for, their shopping cart, and their previous browsing history.

- **News Websites**: News sites like CNN or BBC dynamically display the latest headlines, breaking news, and user comments. As the site is updated, content changes constantly, allowing users to see new articles or information in real-time.

- **Blogs**: WordPress-powered blogs are another example of dynamic websites. When a user adds a comment or a new post, the content of the website is updated dynamically without requiring manual updates from the website administrator.

Dynamic websites are the backbone of modern web applications and provide the functionality needed for users to interact with the site and with each other. They allow for much more flexibility, interactivity, and user engagement than static websites.

# Importance of Server-Side Programming

While HTML, CSS, and JavaScript are often the first technologies that come to mind when building websites, server-side programming languages like PHP play a crucial role in making websites dynamic. Server-side programming allows the website to handle user input, interact with databases, and generate custom responses for each visitor.

### What is Server-Side Programming?

Server-side programming refers to the code that runs on a web server, as opposed to client-side code, which runs in the browser on a user's device. Server-side code is responsible for processing requests, interacting with databases, and generating the HTML that is sent to the client's browser. When a user submits a form, interacts with a website, or requests a page, server-side programming handles the logic behind the scenes.

- **Server-Side vs. Client-Side**:
  - **Server-Side**: Code executes on the server and can access sensitive information like databases and file systems. It is responsible for generating dynamic content.
  - **Client-Side**: Code (typically JavaScript) runs on the client's device and controls how the page looks and behaves. It can respond to user actions like clicks and form submissions but doesn't handle data storage or server communication directly.

Server-side programming languages like PHP are necessary for building dynamic websites because they can process complex tasks that client-side languages like JavaScript cannot. They can manage user authentication, interact with databases to retrieve and store data, and provide functionality like user registration, form submissions, or real-time updates.

# The Role of PHP and MySQL in Building Dynamic Websites

In this book, we will focus on two key technologies: **PHP** and **MySQL**. Together, these technologies form the foundation for building dynamic, data-driven websites.

**PHP: A Powerful Server-Side Language**

PHP is a widely used server-side scripting language designed for web development. It is open-source and integrates seamlessly with MySQL, making it a perfect choice for building dynamic websites. PHP allows you to interact with databases, manage user sessions, handle form submissions, and create dynamic content for websites.

- **Why Use PHP?**
    - **Widely Supported**: PHP is supported by most web hosting services and integrates easily with MySQL databases.
    - **Open Source**: Being free and open-source, PHP has a large, active community and extensive documentation.
    - **Scalable and Secure**: PHP provides features for building scalable applications, and with the right coding practices, it can also be used to build secure websites.

**MySQL: A Robust Database System**

MySQL is a relational database management system (RDBMS) that stores and organizes data. When paired with PHP, MySQL allows developers to create dynamic websites that store and retrieve data, making it possible to create user accounts, store blog posts, manage product inventories, and much more.

- **Why Use MySQL?**

- o **Fast and Reliable**: MySQL is known for its speed and reliability, making it ideal for high-performance web applications.

- o **Flexible and Scalable**: It can easily handle small websites as well as large-scale applications with millions of users.

- o **SQL Queries**: MySQL uses SQL (Structured Query Language) to manage and retrieve data, which is essential for any dynamic website.

Together, PHP and MySQL enable developers to create dynamic websites that respond to user input, retrieve data from databases, and generate customized content. As we move through the chapters in this book, you'll learn how to use PHP to process server requests, interact with MySQL databases, and create secure, interactive, and scalable websites.

# Overview of the Book's Structure

This book is designed to take you through the entire process of building dynamic websites with PHP and MySQL, from the basics to more advanced topics. It's structured to provide hands-on experience with real-world examples, so you can apply what you learn in practical scenarios.

Here's a brief overview of what you can expect:

1. **Introduction to PHP and MySQL**: We'll start by covering the basics of PHP and MySQL, including installation, setup, and basic scripts.

2. **Database Basics**: You'll learn how to design databases, create tables, and write SQL queries to interact with MySQL databases.

3. **Building Dynamic Content**: We'll show you how to use PHP to create dynamic content, process forms, and manage user data.

4. **User Authentication and Security**: You'll learn how to implement secure login systems, session management, and protection against common security threats.

5. **Advanced Features and Performance Optimization**: As we progress, we'll dive into more advanced topics like database optimization, scaling your applications, and using PHP frameworks like Laravel.

6. **Deployment and Maintenance**: Finally, we'll guide you through the process of deploying your dynamic website and maintaining it for long-term success.

---

# Setting Expectations for Security and Scalability

As you learn to build dynamic websites, it's crucial to set expectations for security and scalability from the start.

These two aspects are often overlooked by beginners, but they are vital to the success of any real-world web application.

## Why Security Matters

Security is critical in web development because websites often handle sensitive data such as user credentials, personal information, and payment details. A single security vulnerability can compromise not just the website but also its users.

- **Common Security Threats**:
    - **SQL Injection**: Attackers inject malicious SQL code into form inputs to manipulate the database.
    - **Cross-Site Scripting (XSS)**: Attackers inject malicious scripts into web pages viewed by other users.
    - **Cross-Site Request Forgery (CSRF)**: Attackers trick users into performing actions they didn't intend to.

Throughout this book, we will emphasize security best practices to help you build secure websites that protect both your users and your data.

## Why Scalability Matters

Scalability refers to the ability of your website to handle increased traffic, larger databases, and more complex user interactions as it grows. Websites that are not built with scalability in mind can quickly become slow or unresponsive under heavy loads.

- **Scalability Considerations**:
    - o **Database Optimization**: Efficient queries, indexing, and caching can help your website scale.
    - o **Server Load Balancing**: As your website grows, you may need to distribute traffic across multiple servers.

By the end of this book, you'll have a solid understanding of how to design secure, scalable websites that can handle growth and meet the needs of real-world projects.

---

This book will take you through every step of the process, from building basic dynamic websites with PHP and MySQL to securing and optimizing them for real-world use. By the end, you'll have the skills needed to create professional websites that are secure, scalable, and ready for deployment. So, let's get started on your journey to mastering PHP and MySQL!

# Chapter 1: Introduction to PHP and MySQL

In this chapter, we will take our first steps into the world of dynamic web development by introducing two core technologies: PHP and MySQL. These are the building blocks for creating dynamic, database-driven websites. By the end of this chapter, you'll have a solid understanding of both technologies, how to set up a development environment, and how to write and run your first PHP script. Let's dive in!

---

## What is PHP?

### History, Purpose, and Evolution of PHP

PHP (Hypertext Preprocessor) is a widely-used open-source server-side scripting language designed for web development. It was created by Danish-Canadian programmer Rasmus Lerdorf in 1993, originally as a simple set of Common Gateway Interface (CGI) scripts that tracked visits to his online resume. Over time, PHP grew in scope, adding features for interacting with databases and generating dynamic content. In 1995, Lerdorf released PHP publicly, and it quickly became one of the most popular languages for building dynamic websites.

Initially, PHP stood for "Personal Home Page," but as its features expanded, it was rebranded to "PHP: Hypertext Preprocessor," which is a recursive acronym. The evolution of PHP has been marked by the development of new versions that introduced better features for security, performance, and functionality. From simple page generation to full-fledged web applications, PHP now powers more than 79% of all websites today, including some of the world's most visited platforms such as Facebook, Wikipedia, and WordPress.

**Key Milestones in PHP's Evolution**:

- **PHP 3 (1998)**: The release of PHP 3 introduced an improved architecture and support for object-oriented programming (OOP).

- **PHP 4 (2000)**: Added better performance, support for more databases, and introduced the Zend Engine, a core execution engine that is still in use today.

- **PHP 5 (2004)**: Major enhancements to OOP, the introduction of the PDO (PHP Data Objects) extension, and improvements in XML and web services.

- **PHP 7 (2015)**: Introduced major performance improvements, error handling, and reduced memory consumption, making PHP faster and more scalable than ever.

- **PHP 8 (2020)**: Brought many new features, including Just-In-Time (JIT) compilation, which can significantly improve performance in certain use cases.

## PHP in Real-World Projects

PHP plays a central role in web development, particularly for server-side scripting. It is used to process user requests, interact with databases, and generate dynamic content. Some common use cases of PHP include:

- **Content Management Systems (CMS)**: Platforms like WordPress, Joomla, and Drupal are powered by PHP. These systems allow users to create, manage, and modify content on a website with ease.

- **E-Commerce Websites**: PHP is commonly used to build online stores and marketplaces (like WooCommerce and Magento) that need to interact with databases to store product information, manage users, and process transactions.

- **Social Media Platforms**: Websites like Facebook and Instagram were initially built with PHP, though they have since incorporated other languages. However, PHP still plays a key role in their backend functionality.

- **Web Applications**: PHP is also used to develop a wide range of web applications, including online banking systems, content-sharing platforms, and customer relationship management (CRM) systems.

PHP's ease of use, flexibility, and extensive community support make it a preferred choice for building dynamic websites and web applications.

# What is MySQL?

## Introduction to Databases and MySQL as a Relational Database

MySQL is an open-source relational database management system (RDBMS) that uses Structured Query Language (SQL) to manage and manipulate data. It is one of the most widely used databases in the world, particularly in web development.

A **database** is essentially a collection of data organized in a way that makes it easy to retrieve, update, and manage. In the context of websites, databases store all the data necessary for dynamic websites to function—user profiles, posts, orders, and more.

MySQL is classified as a **relational database**, which means it stores data in tables (also called relations). These tables are organized into rows and columns, where each row represents a record, and each column represents a field of data. The relationships between tables are defined using **foreign keys**, which allow data to be linked across multiple tables.

## Why MySQL?

- **Open Source**: MySQL is free to use and has been maintained by an active community of developers. It has also been part of the popular **LAMP stack** (Linux, Apache, MySQL, PHP/Python/Perl) for many years.

- **Scalability**: MySQL can handle everything from small websites with low traffic to large-scale applications that serve millions of users.

- **Performance**: MySQL is designed to handle high-traffic websites and complex queries efficiently. It supports indexing, caching, and optimized query execution, ensuring fast performance.

- **Security**: MySQL offers robust security features, such as user authentication, access control, and data encryption.

**Real-World Examples of MySQL Usage in Websites**

MySQL is integral to many of the world's most successful websites and web applications. Some of the real-world examples include:

- **Facebook**: While Facebook has evolved into a more complex infrastructure, MySQL was originally used to manage the massive amounts of data related to user accounts, posts, and interactions.

- **YouTube**: MySQL is used to store video metadata, user information, and other data that makes YouTube a dynamic platform.

- **Twitter**: Twitter relies on MySQL for managing user data, tweets, and interactions.

- **E-Commerce Platforms**: Platforms like Magento and WooCommerce use MySQL to manage product inventories, customer data, and transactions.

MySQL is an essential technology for building any website that requires data storage, retrieval, and management.

# Setting Up a Development Environment

Before you can begin writing PHP scripts or interacting with MySQL databases, you'll need to set up a local development environment. This environment will allow you to run PHP and MySQL on your own computer without needing a live web server.

**Installing PHP and MySQL Locally with XAMPP/WAMP**

To get started, you can use a package like **XAMPP** or **WAMP**, both of which are free, open-source software bundles that include Apache, MySQL, and PHP. These packages make it easy to install and configure the components needed to develop dynamic websites on your local machine.

- **XAMPP**: XAMPP stands for Cross-Platform (X), Apache (A), MySQL (M), PHP (P), and Perl (P). It is available for Windows, macOS, and Linux. You can download XAMPP from https://www.apachefriends.org/index.html.

- **WAMP**: WAMP (Windows, Apache, MySQL, PHP) is another popular option for Windows users. It can be downloaded from http://www.wampserver.com/en/.

Once you download and install one of these packages, you'll have a fully functional web server (Apache) and database server (MySQL) running locally on your computer.

### Introduction to PHPMyAdmin for Database Management

After installing XAMPP or WAMP, you can access **PHPMyAdmin**, a web-based application that allows you to manage MySQL databases through a graphical interface. PHPMyAdmin simplifies the process of creating, managing, and manipulating databases, making it an essential tool for developers working with MySQL.

- **Accessing PHPMyAdmin**: Once XAMPP or WAMP is installed, open your browser and go to http://localhost/phpmyadmin. You'll be able to log in with the default credentials and start managing databases.

Through PHPMyAdmin, you can create tables, run SQL queries, import and export data, and manage users.

---

# Your First PHP Script

Now that you have set up your development environment and learned about the technologies, it's time to write and run your first PHP script.

### Writing Your First PHP Script

PHP scripts are typically embedded within HTML files. The PHP code is enclosed within <?php and ?> tags. Here's an example of a very simple PHP script:

php

```php
<?php

echo "Hello, World!";

?>
```

- **Explanation**:
  - `<?php` and `?>` denote the start and end of PHP code.
  - The echo statement is used to output text to the browser.
  - When this script is executed on a web server, it will display "Hello, World!" in the browser.

## Running Your First PHP Script

To run your script, follow these steps:

1. Create a new file in your XAMPP or WAMP directory and name it index.php.

2. Paste the PHP code above into the file.

3. Save the file and navigate to http://localhost/index.php in your browser.

4. If everything is set up correctly, you should see "Hello, World!" displayed in your browser.

---

In this chapter, we've covered the fundamentals of PHP and MySQL, explored their history and real-world applications, and set up a local development environment using XAMPP or WAMP. You've also written and executed your first PHP script, marking the beginning of your journey into dynamic web development.

In the next chapter, we will dive deeper into MySQL, learning how to create and manage databases, tables, and records, as well as how to use SQL queries to interact with data. But for now, take a moment to reflect on the tools and knowledge you've acquired—this is the foundation upon which you'll build your web development skills.

# Chapter 2:
# Understanding the Basics of Server-Side Programming

In this chapter, we will explore the foundations of server-side programming, focusing on how it fits into the process of building dynamic websites with PHP. We will cover what server-side programming is, how PHP operates on the server, and the critical differences between client-side and server-side code. Additionally, we will explore how PHP handles HTTP requests and demonstrates how forms and user input are processed by the server. This will lay the groundwork for building dynamic websites that respond to user interaction.

## What is Server-Side Programming?

Server-side programming refers to the code that runs on the server, as opposed to the client's browser (client-side). When a user interacts with a website, certain operations—such as retrieving data from a database, sending an email, or processing sensitive information—must be handled securely and efficiently on the server. Server-side programming is responsible for these tasks.

In the context of web development, server-side programming involves writing scripts that run on the server in response to user requests. The server processes the requests, performs necessary actions (such as querying a database or performing calculations), and then sends back a response to the client, typically in the form of HTML, CSS, and JavaScript.

Some examples of server-side programming languages include:

- **PHP**: A popular scripting language for web development, often used for interacting with databases and generating dynamic content.

- **Python (with frameworks like Django and Flask)**: Used for building web applications with server-side logic.

- **Ruby (with Ruby on Rails)**: A language that emphasizes convention over configuration for building web applications.

- **Java (with frameworks like Spring)**: Used in enterprise-level applications, especially for large-scale systems.

In this chapter, we will focus on **PHP**, a server-side language that is widely used for building dynamic websites.

### Why is Server-Side Programming Important?

Server-side programming is essential because it allows websites to offer interactive and personalized experiences. Some critical tasks that server-side programming handles include:

- **Database Interaction**: PHP can be used to connect to databases, retrieve records, and display data dynamically.

- **Authentication and Authorization**: User login systems and permissions management are typically handled server-side to maintain security.

- **Data Processing**: Operations such as processing form submissions, calculations, and file uploads happen on the server.

- **Handling Business Logic**: PHP handles the core functionality of applications by implementing complex algorithms, workflows, and interactions between different systems.

Without server-side programming, websites would be static, unable to respond to user input in meaningful ways. Server-side programming enables the dynamic nature of modern websites, such as e-commerce sites, social media platforms, and online banking.

---

## How PHP Works on the Server

PHP is a server-side scripting language, which means that when a user requests a webpage that contains PHP code, the server processes the PHP code and sends back the resulting HTML, CSS, and JavaScript to the client's browser. PHP itself is never visible to the user—it only exists on the server to handle specific requests and deliver a response.

Here's how PHP works step by step:

1. **Request**: A user sends a request to access a webpage (for example, http://example.com/profile.php).

2. **Server Processing**: The web server (Apache, Nginx, etc.) sees that the file has a .php extension and passes it to the PHP engine.

3. **Execution**: The PHP engine processes the PHP code, which may involve reading from a database, performing calculations, or interacting with other systems. During this process, any echo or print statements in the PHP code output HTML to be sent to the client.

4. **Response**: Once the PHP code has been executed, the resulting HTML is sent back to the browser, where it is rendered for the user to view.

5. **Display**: The user sees the result, which could be anything from a simple text message to a fully interactive web page with dynamic content.

In short, PHP is used to generate dynamic content, handle requests from the user, and respond with HTML, which the client's browser then interprets.

**Example of PHP Execution**

To better understand the flow, let's walk through a simple example of how PHP executes code:

1. A user navigates to http://localhost/greeting.php.

2. The server processes the file greeting.php, which contains the following PHP code:

php

```php
<?php
    echo "Hello, welcome to our website!";
?>
```

3. The PHP code is executed on the server, and the string "Hello, welcome to our website!" is output to the browser as HTML.

4. The browser displays the message as part of the webpage.

In this process, PHP has generated the response dynamically based on the script it ran, while the client simply receives the result as HTML.

---

# Difference Between Client-Side and Server-Side Code

Understanding the distinction between client-side and server-side code is fundamental to web development. While both are necessary for building dynamic websites, they serve different purposes and run in different locations.

**Client-Side Code:**

- **Location**: Runs in the user's browser.
- **Languages Used**: HTML, CSS, JavaScript.

- **Responsibilities**: Responsible for rendering the webpage's content and enabling user interactions within the browser (e.g., clicking buttons, animations, form validation).

- **Visibility**: The user can view and interact with client-side code in the browser's developer tools (JavaScript, HTML, and CSS).

- **Execution**: Runs when the page is loaded and continuously as the user interacts with the page (e.g., JavaScript reacts to events like mouse clicks or form submissions).

For example, JavaScript can be used to update the content of a page without needing to refresh the entire page (AJAX). It provides rich user interfaces and is ideal for things like validating form data before sending it to the server.

**Server-Side Code:**

- **Location**: Runs on the web server, not in the browser.

- **Languages Used**: PHP, Python, Ruby, Java, Node.js, etc.

- **Responsibilities**: Handles the core functionality, like interacting with a database, processing form submissions, generating dynamic content, and managing authentication and authorization.

- **Visibility**: The user cannot see server-side code—it is executed on the server, and only the final HTML response is visible in the browser.

- **Execution**: Server-side code executes only when a user requests a specific page or submits a form, and it typically generates a new HTML page to be sent back to the client.

In summary, client-side code handles user interface aspects, while server-side code handles the logic and data processing. They work together to create dynamic and interactive websites.

---

# How PHP Handles HTTP Requests

When a user interacts with a website, they send HTTP requests to the server. These requests can be triggered by various actions, such as visiting a URL, submitting a form, or clicking a link. PHP is responsible for processing these requests, performing any necessary operations, and sending an appropriate response.

### HTTP Request Flow with PHP

Here's an example of how PHP handles an HTTP request in a typical workflow:

1. **User Request**: The user fills out a form on a webpage (e.g., a login form) and clicks the submit button. This triggers an HTTP POST request to the server, containing the form data.

2. **Server Receives Request**: The server receives the HTTP request and processes it based on the URL and method (GET, POST, etc.). If the request is

directed to a PHP script, the server passes the request to the PHP engine.

3. **PHP Processes Request**: PHP extracts the form data from the request (such as the username and password), performs necessary operations (e.g., checking the database for matching credentials), and prepares a response.

4. **Response**: After processing, PHP may generate a new page with a welcome message or an error message, which is then sent back to the user's browser as an HTML response.

5. **User Sees Response**: The user sees the response in their browser, such as a successful login message or a prompt to retry with the correct credentials.

PHP's ability to receive, process, and respond to HTTP requests is at the heart of server-side programming. It is through this process that PHP enables dynamic content generation and interaction with databases.

# The Role of Forms and User Input

Forms are the primary way users interact with websites. When a user submits a form, the data is sent to the server where it is processed. PHP is used to handle the submission, validate the input, and perform any necessary operations (such as storing the data in a database).

### Simple Form Submission and Processing with PHP

Let's go through an example of a simple form submission using PHP. Consider a basic contact form where users can enter their name and email address:

html

```
<form action="process.php" method="POST">
    <label for="name">Name:</label>
    <input type="text" name="name" id="name" required>

    <label for="email">Email:</label>
    <input type="email" name="email" id="email" required>

    <input type="submit" value="Submit">
</form>
```

- **Form Action**: The action attribute specifies the file (process.php) where the form data will be sent when submitted.

- **Form Method**: The method="POST" indicates that the data will be sent using the POST HTTP method, which is more secure than GET for transmitting sensitive information.

In the process.php file, PHP can process the form data as follows:

php

```php
<?php
    if ($_SERVER["REQUEST_METHOD"] == "POST") {
        $name = $_POST['name'];
        $email = $_POST['email'];

        // Process the form data (e.g., store it in a database)
        echo "Thank you, $name! We will contact you at $email.";
    }
?>
```

Here, PHP retrieves the form data using $_POST (which is a global associative array containing data sent via the POST method). The data can then be used in further operations, such as storing it in a database, sending an email, or performing validation.

Server-side programming is a crucial part of building dynamic, interactive websites. PHP plays a central role in handling requests, processing user input, and generating dynamic content. Understanding how PHP works on the server, how it processes HTTP requests, and how to handle forms and user input will provide you with the necessary skills to start building your own dynamic websites. As we continue through this book, we'll build on these fundamentals and dive deeper into more advanced topics related to security, scalability, and working with databases.

# Chapter 3: Introduction to Databases

In this chapter, we will dive into the world of databases, focusing on relational databases and MySQL, a popular database management system. A fundamental part of building dynamic websites is the ability to store, retrieve, and manipulate data. Databases play a crucial role in this process by providing an organized way to store information and enabling efficient access to that data. We'll cover the essential concepts of databases, SQL (Structured Query Language), and how to work with MySQL to manage your data effectively.

---

## What is a Database?

A **database** is a structured collection of data that is stored and managed in a way that allows for efficient access, management, and updating. The goal of a database is to store data in an organized manner so that it can be easily retrieved, modified, and deleted when necessary.

In a modern web application, databases are used to store various types of data, such as user profiles, product information, posts, comments, orders, and more. These data types are typically organized into tables, with each table containing rows (records) and columns (attributes or fields).

The most common type of database is a **relational database**, which organizes data into tables with relationships between them. Relational databases are widely used due to their efficiency and the power of SQL, which allows for complex queries and data manipulation.

**Key Characteristics of a Database:**

- **Data Organization**: Data is structured in tables, which are composed of rows and columns. Each table has a unique name.

- **Data Integrity**: Ensures the data stored is accurate and consistent.

- **Data Access**: Allows for fast and efficient querying of data.

- **Data Security**: Provides mechanisms for controlling access and ensuring data is protected.

---

# Introduction to Relational Databases

A **relational database** stores data in tables that are related to each other through keys. These tables have columns that define the attributes of the data (such as "Name," "Email," or "Price") and rows that represent individual records. The power of relational databases lies in their ability to define relationships between tables and perform complex queries.

**Key Concepts in Relational Databases:**

- **Tables**: These are collections of data organized by rows and columns. Each table is designed to store information on a particular entity or object.

- **Primary Keys**: A primary key is a unique identifier for each row in a table. For example, in a table of users, the user_id could be the primary key.

- **Foreign Keys**: A foreign key is a column in one table that references the primary key of another table, establishing a relationship between the two tables.

- **Normalization**: The process of designing a database schema to reduce data redundancy and ensure that the data is stored in a logical and efficient manner.

For example, in an e-commerce website, you might have a table for products and a table for orders. The orders table might contain a product_id column that references the product_id in the products table, establishing a relationship between the two tables.

# Overview of SQL (Structured Query Language)

SQL (Structured Query Language) is the language used to interact with relational databases. It allows you to create, modify, and query data within a database. SQL is an essential tool for any database administrator or developer working with relational databases.

**Common SQL Commands:**

- **CREATE**: Used to create a new database or table.

- **SELECT**: Used to retrieve data from one or more tables.

- **INSERT**: Used to add new data (records) into a table.

- **UPDATE**: Used to modify existing records in a table.

- **DELETE**: Used to remove records from a table.

SQL is known for its simple, English-like syntax. Even though it's a powerful tool, it is quite intuitive once you understand the basic structure and commands.

Here are some examples of SQL commands:

- **SELECT**: Retrieves data from one or more tables.

sql

```
SELECT * FROM users;
```

This command retrieves all columns and rows from the users table.

- **INSERT**: Adds new data to a table.

sql

```
INSERT INTO users (name, email) VALUES ('John Doe', 'johndoe@example.com');
```

This command adds a new user to the users table with the name "John Doe" and email address "johndoe@example.com."

- **UPDATE**: Modifies existing records in a table.

sql

```
UPDATE users SET email = 'newemail@example.com' WHERE name = 'John Doe';
```

This command updates the email address for the user "John Doe."

- **DELETE**: Removes records from a table.

sql

```
DELETE FROM users WHERE name = 'John Doe';
```

This command deletes the user "John Doe" from the users table.

---

# Creating a Database with MySQL

MySQL is one of the most popular relational database management systems (RDBMS) used for web applications. MySQL allows developers to easily create and manage databases, tables, and data. It is open-source, fast, and widely used in the web development community, particularly with PHP for server-side scripting.

### Setting Up MySQL:

1. **Install MySQL**: If you haven't already installed MySQL, you can download it from the official MySQL website and follow the installation instructions. Many developers use packages like **XAMPP** or **WAMP**, which provide both PHP and MySQL in a single installation.

2. **Accessing MySQL**: Once MySQL is installed, you can access it through a command-line interface or a GUI tool like **PHPMyAdmin**, which simplifies database management through a web interface.

### Creating a Database:

To create a database in MySQL, you can use the CREATE DATABASE command. For example:

sql

CREATE DATABASE my_blog;

This command creates a new database called my_blog.

### Using a Database:

Once a database is created, you need to select it before creating tables or manipulating data. Use the USE command to select a database:

sql

USE my_blog;

After selecting a database, you can create tables, insert data, and run queries.

---

# Simple SQL Queries (CREATE, SELECT, INSERT)

Once you have a database set up, you can begin creating tables to store your data. Here are some basic SQL queries that will help you get started:

**Creating a Table:**

A table is a collection of columns and rows. To create a table, you need to define the table name, columns, and data types for each column. Here is an example of creating a table for a blog:

sql

```sql
CREATE TABLE posts (
    post_id INT AUTO_INCREMENT PRIMARY KEY,
    title VARCHAR(255) NOT NULL,
    content TEXT NOT NULL,
    author_id INT,
    created_at TIMESTAMP DEFAULT CURRENT_TIMESTAMP
);
```

In this example:

- The post_id column is an **integer** and the primary key for the table. It automatically increments with each new post.

- The title column is a **string** (VARCHAR), and it cannot be null.

- The content column is a **text** field, used for the body of the post.

- The author_id column is an integer that could be used to reference a user table.

- The created_at column stores the timestamp when the post was created.

**Inserting Data into a Table:**

After creating the table, you can insert data into it using the INSERT statement:

sql

```
INSERT INTO posts (title, content, author_id)

VALUES ('My First Post', 'This is the content of the post', 1);
```

This command adds a new post with the title "My First Post" and content "This is the content of the post" to the posts table. The author_id is set to 1, referencing the author of the post.

**Selecting Data from a Table:**

To retrieve data from the table, you can use the SELECT statement. For example:

sql

```
SELECT * FROM posts;
```

This retrieves all columns for all posts in the posts table.

If you want to retrieve specific columns, you can modify the query:

sql

```
SELECT title, content FROM posts;
```

This will only retrieve the title and content columns for each post.

---

# Working with Tables in MySQL

In this section, we'll discuss how to manage tables and their relationships in MySQL. The relationships between tables are central to the relational database model.

### Defining Relationships with Foreign Keys:

You can create relationships between tables by using **foreign keys**. For example, let's say you have a users table and a posts table. Each post is authored by a user, so the posts table might include a user_id column that references the user_id in the users table.

sql

```sql
CREATE TABLE users (
    user_id INT AUTO_INCREMENT PRIMARY KEY,
    username VARCHAR(255) NOT NULL,
    email VARCHAR(255) NOT NULL
);

CREATE TABLE posts (
    post_id INT AUTO_INCREMENT PRIMARY KEY,
    title VARCHAR(255) NOT NULL,
    content TEXT NOT NULL,
    user_id INT,
    FOREIGN KEY (user_id) REFERENCES users(user_id)
);
```

In this example, the user_id in the posts table is a foreign key that references the user_id in the users table. This enforces the relationship between the two tables, ensuring that each post is associated with a valid user.

# Real-World Examples of Tables for a Blog or E-Commerce Site

1. **Blog**:

   - **Users Table**: Stores user information such as usernames, email addresses, and passwords.

   - **Posts Table**: Stores the content of blog posts, titles, authors, and timestamps.

   - **Comments Table**: Stores comments related to each post, including the commenter's user ID, the post ID, and the content of the comment.

2. **E-Commerce Site**:

   - **Products Table**: Stores information about products, such as names, descriptions, prices, and stock quantities.

   - **Orders Table**: Stores customer orders, including product IDs, customer information, and order details.

   - **Customers Table**: Stores customer data, including names, shipping addresses, and payment details.

---

In this chapter, we explored the fundamentals of databases, focusing on relational databases and MySQL. We learned how to create and manage databases, write SQL queries to interact with them, and define relationships between tables. Understanding how to work with databases is essential for building dynamic websites that require data storage and retrieval, such as blogs or e-commerce sites.

# Chapter 4: Connecting PHP to MySQL

In this chapter, we will dive into the process of connecting PHP to MySQL databases. Understanding how to connect to a database, run queries, and retrieve data is essential for building dynamic websites. We'll explore the two primary methods PHP uses to communicate with MySQL: **MySQLi** (MySQL Improved) and **PDO** (PHP Data Objects). Both of these methods allow you to interact with MySQL databases, but they offer different features and use cases.

We'll also walk through basic PHP scripts to connect to a MySQL database, perform queries, and display data dynamically on a webpage.

---

## How PHP Connects to MySQL

PHP connects to MySQL databases using an extension that provides functions for performing SQL operations. Two popular extensions for database interaction are **MySQLi** and **PDO**. Each of these has its advantages and is suitable for different use cases.

### MySQLi (MySQL Improved)

MySQLi is a PHP extension specifically designed for interacting with MySQL databases. It is called "improved" because it offers several enhancements over the original

MySQL extension, including support for prepared statements, object-oriented programming (OOP) style, and the ability to handle multiple statements.

MySQLi supports two styles:

1. **Procedural Style**: Uses function calls to interact with the database.

2. **Object-Oriented Style (OOP)**: Uses classes and objects to interact with the database.

**PDO (PHP Data Objects)**

PDO is a more general-purpose extension that supports multiple database management systems, not just MySQL. It is designed to provide a uniform interface for interacting with various databases, including MySQL, PostgreSQL, SQLite, and others.

PDO uses a consistent API across different databases and provides more flexibility in working with different types of databases. It also supports prepared statements for security and performance improvements.

---

# Introduction to the MySQLi and PDO Extensions in PHP

**Using MySQLi:**

To connect to MySQL with MySQLi, you need to use the mysqli_connect() function for procedural style or create an instance of the mysqli class for object-oriented style. Let's first look at how to do this in procedural style.

**MySQLi Procedural Style**:

php

```php
<?php
// Database connection parameters
$host = 'localhost';
$username = 'root';
$password = '';
$dbname = 'my_blog';

// Establish connection
$conn = mysqli_connect($host, $username, $password, $dbname);

// Check connection
if (!$conn) {
    die("Connection failed: " . mysqli_connect_error());
}
echo "Connected successfully";
?>
```

Here, we use mysqli_connect() to establish a connection to the database. If the connection fails, we use mysqli_connect_error() to print out an error message. If the connection is successful, it prints a success message.

**MySQLi Object-Oriented Style**:

php

```php
<?php
// Database connection parameters
$host = 'localhost';
$username = 'root';
$password = '';
$dbname = 'my_blog';

// Create a new mysqli object
$conn = new mysqli($host, $username, $password, $dbname);

// Check connection
if ($conn->connect_error) {
    die("Connection failed: " . $conn->connect_error);
}
echo "Connected successfully";
?>
```

In this version, we create a new instance of the mysqli class and use its connect_error property to check if there was a problem connecting to the database.

**Using PDO:**

PDO is a more flexible way to interact with databases in PHP. It allows you to work with different database systems with the same set of functions. Here's how to connect to MySQL using PDO:

php

```php
<?php
// Database connection parameters
$host = 'localhost';

$username = 'root';

$password = '';

$dbname = 'my_blog';


try {
    // Create a new PDO instance

    $conn = new PDO("mysql:host=$host;dbname=$dbname", $username, $password);


    // Set the PDO error mode to exception
```

```
$conn->setAttribute(PDO::ATTR_ERRMODE,
PDO::ERRMODE_EXCEPTION);

    echo "Connected successfully";

}

catch(PDOException $e) {

    echo "Connection failed: " . $e->getMessage();

}

?>
```

In the PDO example, we use the new PDO() constructor to create a connection. We also set the ATTR_ERRMODE attribute to handle errors by throwing exceptions, which can be caught in the catch block.

**When to Use MySQLi vs. PDO:**

- **Use MySQLi** when you are only working with MySQL databases and you want the performance benefits and features specific to MySQL, such as support for multiple queries and prepared statements.

- **Use PDO** if you need to support multiple database systems, as it provides a consistent API across different databases.

# Writing Simple PHP Scripts to Connect to a Database

Once we've established the connection, we can write PHP scripts to interact with the database, run SQL queries, and display the results. Let's go through a basic example of how to retrieve and display data from a MySQL database.

**Fetching Data from MySQL:**

Suppose we have a database called my_blog with a posts table that stores blog posts. The table might look something like this:

sql

```
CREATE TABLE posts (
    post_id INT AUTO_INCREMENT PRIMARY KEY,
    title VARCHAR(255) NOT NULL,
    content TEXT NOT NULL,
    created_at TIMESTAMP DEFAULT CURRENT_TIMESTAMP
);
```

Now, let's write a PHP script that connects to the database and fetches all posts from the posts table.

**Using MySQLi (Procedural Style):**

php

```php
<?php
// Database connection parameters
$host = 'localhost';
$username = 'root';
$password = '';
$dbname = 'my_blog';

// Establish connection
$conn = mysqli_connect($host, $username, $password, $dbname);

// Check connection
if (!$conn) {
    die("Connection failed: " . mysqli_connect_error());
}

// Query to fetch data from the posts table
$query = "SELECT * FROM posts";
$result = mysqli_query($conn, $query);

// Display the data
if (mysqli_num_rows($result) > 0) {
```

```php
    while ($row = mysqli_fetch_assoc($result)) {

        echo "<h2>" . $row['title'] . "</h2>";

        echo "<p>" . $row['content'] . "</p>";

        echo "<small>Posted on: " . $row['created_at'] .
"</small><hr>";

    }
} else {

    echo "No posts found.";

}


// Close the connection

mysqli_close($conn);

?>
```

In this example:

- We use mysqli_query() to execute the SELECT query and fetch all records from the posts table.

- We use mysqli_fetch_assoc() to fetch each row of the result as an associative array, which we then display dynamically using HTML.

**Using PDO**:

php


```php
<?php
```

```php
// Database connection parameters
$host = 'localhost';
$username = 'root';
$password = '';
$dbname = 'my_blog';


try {
    // Create a new PDO instance
    $conn = new
PDO("mysql:host=$host;dbname=$dbname", $username,
$password);


    // Set the PDO error mode to exception
    $conn->setAttribute(PDO::ATTR_ERRMODE,
PDO::ERRMODE_EXCEPTION);


    // Query to fetch data from the posts table
    $query = "SELECT * FROM posts";
    $stmt = $conn->query($query);


    // Display the data
    while ($row = $stmt->fetch(PDO::FETCH_ASSOC)) {
        echo "<h2>" . $row['title'] . "</h2>";
```

```php
        echo "<p>" . $row['content'] . "</p>";

        echo "<small>Posted on: " . $row['created_at'] .
"</small><hr>";

    }

} catch (PDOException $e) {

    echo "Error: " . $e->getMessage();

}

?>
```

In the PDO example:

- We use the query() method to execute the SQL query and fetch all rows.

- The fetch() method retrieves each row as an associative array (PDO::FETCH_ASSOC), and we display the data in the same way.

# Displaying Data Dynamically on a Webpage

Now that you know how to retrieve data from the database, the next step is to display it dynamically on a webpage. This is achieved by embedding the PHP code inside HTML.

**Example: Displaying Blog Posts Dynamically**

Let's put everything together to display blog posts dynamically on a webpage. Here's how the complete page might look:

php

```php
<!DOCTYPE html>
<html lang="en">
<head>
    <meta charset="UTF-8">
    <meta name="viewport" content="width=device-width, initial-scale=1.0">
    <title>Blog Posts</title>
</head>
<body>

<h1>Latest Blog Posts</h1>

<?php
// Database connection parameters
$host = 'localhost';
$username = 'root';
$password = '';
$dbname = 'my_blog';
```

```php
try {
    // Create a new PDO instance
    $conn = new PDO("mysql:host=$host;dbname=$dbname", $username, $password);

    // Set the PDO error mode to exception
    $conn->setAttribute(PDO::ATTR_ERRMODE, PDO::ERRMODE_EXCEPTION);

    // Query to fetch data from the posts table
    $query = "SELECT * FROM posts ORDER BY created_at DESC";
    $stmt = $conn->query($query);

    // Display the data
    while ($row = $stmt->fetch(PDO::FETCH_ASSOC)) {
        echo "<h2>" . $row['title'] . "</h2>";
        echo "<p>" . $row['content'] . "</p>";
        echo "<small>Posted on: " . $row['created_at'] . "</small><hr>";
    }
} catch (PDOException $e) {
```

```
    echo "Error: " . $e->getMessage();

}

?>
```

```
</body>

</html>
```

This webpage will display the blog posts dynamically, with each post's title, content, and creation date pulled from the MySQL database.

---

In this chapter, we learned how to connect PHP to MySQL using both **MySQLi** and **PDO** extensions. We explored how to write PHP scripts to connect to the database, run SQL queries, fetch data, and display it dynamically on a webpage. These skills are foundational for building dynamic, data-driven websites like blogs, e-commerce sites, and content management systems. As we move forward, we will build on this knowledge to create more advanced functionality, such as inserting, updating, and deleting data from the database.

# Chapter 5: Creating and Managing Forms in PHP

In this chapter, we will explore how to create and manage forms in PHP, focusing on user input handling, validation, and storing data in a MySQL database. Forms are essential elements of dynamic websites, allowing users to interact with the site, submit data, and trigger actions. PHP is commonly used to process and validate the data submitted through forms, and it allows you to store that data in a database for later retrieval.

---

## HTML Forms and PHP

Forms in HTML provide a way for users to enter data, which can then be processed by the server using PHP. A typical form is created using the <form> element, which contains various input fields like textboxes, radio buttons, checkboxes, and buttons.

### Creating Forms in HTML

To begin, let's look at a simple HTML form. Here's an example of a form that asks the user for their name, email, and password:

html

```html
<!DOCTYPE html>
<html lang="en">
<head>
  <meta charset="UTF-8">
  <meta name="viewport" content="width=device-width,
initial-scale=1.0">
  <title>User Registration Form</title>
</head>
<body>
  <h2>Register</h2>
  <form action="process_form.php" method="POST">
    <label for="name">Name:</label>
    <input type="text" id="name" name="name"
required><br><br>


    <label for="email">Email:</label>
    <input type="email" id="email" name="email"
required><br><br>


    <label for="password">Password:</label>
    <input type="password" id="password"
name="password" required><br><br>
```

```
<input type="submit" value="Register">

   </form>

</body>

</html>
```

- The form uses the POST method, which means the form data will be sent to the server in the body of the HTTP request (rather than as part of the URL, which would happen with the GET method).

- The action attribute specifies the file (process_form.php) that will handle the form data when the form is submitted.

# Handling User Input in PHP

When a user submits a form, the data is sent to a PHP script, where it can be processed. In the example above, the action="process_form.php" attribute directs the form submission to the process_form.php file.

### Accessing Form Data

PHP provides superglobals like $_GET and $_POST to access data submitted by forms using the GET and POST methods, respectively.

- $_POST is used when the form data is sent via the POST method (as in our example above).

- $_GET is used when the form data is sent via the GET method.

Here is an example of how you can access the form data in PHP:

php

```php
<?php
if ($_SERVER["REQUEST_METHOD"] == "POST") {
    // Collect form data
    $name = $_POST['name'];
    $email = $_POST['email'];
    $password = $_POST['password'];

    // Process the data (e.g., store it in the database)
    echo "Name: " . htmlspecialchars($name) . "<br>";
    echo "Email: " . htmlspecialchars($email) . "<br>";
}
?>
```

- **$_POST['name']** accesses the value submitted in the name input field.
- **htmlspecialchars()** is used to escape special characters to prevent XSS (cross-site scripting) attacks.

**GET vs. POST Method**

- **GET Method**: The data is appended to the URL in the form of query parameters. This method is suitable for forms where data is not sensitive and can be displayed in the URL (e.g., search forms).

Example:

html

```
<form action="search_results.php" method="GET">

    <label for="search">Search:</label>

    <input type="text" name="search" required>

    <input type="submit" value="Search">
</form>
```

On submission, the form data is appended to the URL as:

sql

```
search_results.php?search=example
```

- **POST Method**: The data is sent in the body of the HTTP request, making it more secure than GET for sensitive data. This is the method used in forms like login or registration, where sensitive information (such as passwords) is submitted.

# Validating User Input

Input validation is critical for ensuring that the data submitted by users is correct, secure, and in the correct format. Invalid input can result in errors, security vulnerabilities, and database issues.

**Importance of Input Validation**

Some of the reasons why input validation is important:

- **Security**: To prevent attacks such as SQL injection, XSS, and other forms of malicious input.

- **Data Integrity**: To ensure the data entered meets the required format (e.g., a valid email address).

- **User Experience**: To give users immediate feedback when their input is incorrect.

**Validating Email and Password**

Let's validate the email and password inputs in the registration form.

- **Email Validation**: You can use PHP's built-in filter_var() function to validate email addresses.

php

```php
$email = $_POST['email'];
if (!filter_var($email, FILTER_VALIDATE_EMAIL)) {
    echo "Invalid email format.";
} else {
```

```php
echo "Email is valid.";
}
```

- **Password Validation**: A strong password typically requires a combination of uppercase letters, lowercase letters, numbers, and special characters. We can validate this using regular expressions.

php

```php
$password = $_POST['password'];
if (strlen($password) < 8) {
    echo "Password must be at least 8 characters long.";
} elseif (!preg_match("/[A-Z]/", $password)) {
    echo "Password must contain at least one uppercase letter.";
} elseif (!preg_match("/[0-9]/", $password)) {
    echo "Password must contain at least one number.";
} else {
    echo "Password is valid.";
}
```

In this example, the password is validated to ensure it's at least 8 characters long and contains at least one uppercase letter and one number.

**Real-world Example: User Registration Form**

A user registration form collects important user information, including email and password. Below is an example of a basic registration form with email and password validation.

php

```php
<?php
if ($_SERVER["REQUEST_METHOD"] == "POST") {
    // Collect and validate form data
    $name = htmlspecialchars($_POST['name']);
    $email = $_POST['email'];
    $password = $_POST['password'];

    // Validate email
    if (!filter_var($email, FILTER_VALIDATE_EMAIL)) {
        echo "Invalid email format.";
    }
    // Validate password
    elseif (strlen($password) < 8 || !preg_match("/[A-Z]/", $password) || !preg_match("/[0-9]/", $password)) {
        echo "Password must be at least 8 characters long, include one uppercase letter and one number.";
    } else {
        // Store the data (e.g., in a database)
```

```
    echo "Registration successful!";

  }

}
?>
```

This form validates the email and password and then processes the data. If the validation fails, it shows error messages; otherwise, it confirms successful registration.

---

# Form Handling and Storing Data in MySQL

Once the form data is validated, it is usually stored in a database for later use, such as in user registration or submitting blog comments. Let's take a look at how to insert the form data into a MySQL database.

### Inserting Form Data into a Database

Let's consider a scenario where users can leave comments on a blog post. When a user submits a comment, it is stored in the database.

1. **Create a Table for Comments**:

sql

```sql
CREATE TABLE comments (

  comment_id INT AUTO_INCREMENT PRIMARY KEY,
```

```
post_id INT NOT NULL,

user_name VARCHAR(255) NOT NULL,

comment_text TEXT NOT NULL,

created_at TIMESTAMP DEFAULT
CURRENT_TIMESTAMP

);
```

2. **PHP Script to Insert Data into the Database**:

php

```php
<?php
if ($_SERVER["REQUEST_METHOD"] == "POST") {
    // Collect and validate form data
    $post_id = $_POST['post_id'];
    $user_name = htmlspecialchars($_POST['user_name']);
    $comment_text =
htmlspecialchars($_POST['comment_text']);

    // Validate comment text
    if (empty($comment_text)) {
        echo "Comment cannot be empty.";
    } else {
```

```php
// Database connection
$host = 'localhost';

$username = 'root';

$password = '';

$dbname = 'my_blog';


$conn = new
PDO("mysql:host=$host;dbname=$dbname", $username,
$password);

$conn->setAttribute(PDO::ATTR_ERRMODE,
PDO::ERRMODE_EXCEPTION);


// Insert comment into the database

$stmt = $conn->prepare("INSERT INTO comments
(post_id, user_name, comment_text) VALUES (:post_id,
:user_name, :comment_text)");

$stmt->bindParam(':post_id', $post_id);

$stmt->bindParam(':user_name', $user_name);

$stmt->bindParam(':comment_text', $comment_text);


if ($stmt->execute()) {

    echo "Comment added successfully!";

} else {

    echo "Error adding comment.";
```

```
        }

    }

}

?>
```

In this script:

- The form data is collected and validated.

- A connection to the MySQL database is established using PDO.

- The INSERT INTO query is executed to store the comment in the database.

**Real-World Example: Blog Comment Section**

This example shows how a blog post's comment section can be powered by PHP and MySQL. Users submit their names and comments through a form, and the comments are stored in a database. Later, they can be retrieved and displayed dynamically.

---

In this chapter, we explored how to create and manage forms in PHP, focusing on handling user input, validating that input, and storing it in a MySQL database. Form handling is an essential skill in dynamic website development, allowing users to interact with your website and submit data. By validating and sanitizing input, you ensure that your website remains secure, user-friendly, and reliable. With this knowledge, you can create user registration systems, comment sections, contact forms, and much more. As we continue, we'll delve into more advanced topics like session management, security, and working with more complex forms.

# Chapter 6: Working with Sessions and Cookies

In this chapter, we will delve into the concept of sessions and cookies in PHP, both of which are essential for handling user data across multiple requests. These tools allow developers to store temporary and persistent data, manage user authentication, and enhance user experience by remembering user preferences. We will also discuss security practices to ensure that both sessions and cookies are properly secured against common threats like session hijacking and cookie theft.

## What are Sessions?

Sessions are a mechanism for storing user-specific data across multiple pages on a website. Unlike cookies, which are stored on the user's computer, session data is stored on the server. This makes sessions more secure and ideal for handling sensitive data, such as user login information.

When a user accesses a website, a unique session ID is created. This session ID is typically stored in the user's browser as a cookie, and it is sent with each subsequent request to the server. The server uses this session ID to identify the user and retrieve any associated data.

**How PHP Sessions Work**

PHP makes working with sessions simple by providing built-in functions. These functions help create, store, and manage session data. The session data is stored on the server, and only a reference to the data (a session ID) is sent to the user's browser.

Here's how PHP sessions work:

1. **Starting a Session**: Before any session variables can be used, you must start the session using the session_start() function.

2. **Storing Session Data**: Once the session is started, you can store data in the $_SESSION superglobal array.

3. **Retrieving Session Data**: You can access stored session data using the $_SESSION array.

4. **Destroying a Session**: To remove all session data, the session_destroy() function can be called.

# Real-World Example: User Login Session

One of the most common uses of sessions is for user authentication. When a user logs in, you can store information about the user in a session variable, such as their user ID or name. This data can be accessed across different pages of the website, allowing users to remain logged in as they navigate through the site.

Here's an example of how a login system can use sessions:

1. **Login Form** (login.php):

html

```html
<form action="login_process.php" method="POST">
    <label for="username">Username:</label>
    <input type="text" name="username" required><br><br>
    <label for="password">Password:</label>
    <input type="password" name="password" required><br><br>
    <input type="submit" value="Login">
</form>
```

2. **Processing the Login** (login_process.php):

php

```php
<?php
session_start();

// Assuming you already have a way to validate the user (e.g., checking against a database)
if ($_POST['username'] == "user" && $_POST['password'] == "password") {
```

```php
    // Store user data in session variables
    $_SESSION['username'] = $_POST['username'];
    $_SESSION['loggedin'] = true;
    header("Location: dashboard.php");
} else {
    echo "Invalid login credentials.";
}
?>
```

3. **Accessing Session Data** (dashboard.php):

php

```php
<?php
session_start();

if (isset($_SESSION['loggedin']) &&
$_SESSION['loggedin'] === true) {
    echo "Welcome, " . $_SESSION['username'] . "!";
} else {
    echo "You are not logged in. Please <a
href='login.php'>log in</a> first.";
}
?>
```

In this example:

- When the user submits the login form, the PHP script validates the credentials and stores the username and login status in session variables.

- On subsequent pages (like dashboard.php), the session is used to check if the user is logged in and display personalized content.

**Session Timeout**

A common feature of sessions is setting an expiration time to automatically log users out after a period of inactivity. This is often done by checking the last activity timestamp and comparing it with the current time.

Example of session timeout:

php

```php
session_start();


// Set the timeout period (in seconds)
$timeout_duration = 1800; // 30 minutes


// Check if the session has expired
if (isset($_SESSION['last_activity']) && (time() -
$_SESSION['last_activity']) > $timeout_duration) {

    session_unset(); // Unset session variables

    session_destroy(); // Destroy session

    header("Location: login.php"); // Redirect to login page
```

```
}
```

$_SESSION['last_activity'] = time();  // Update last activity timestamp

---

# What are Cookies?

Cookies are small pieces of data that are stored on the user's device. Unlike sessions, which are stored on the server, cookies are stored on the client-side (in the user's browser). They are typically used for storing persistent data such as user preferences, login tokens, or tracking information across sessions.

Cookies are sent along with each HTTP request to the server, making them useful for storing information that should persist between user sessions, such as "remember me" functionality on websites.

**How Cookies Work**

- **Setting a Cookie**: You can set a cookie in PHP using the setcookie() function. This function allows you to specify the cookie name, value, expiration time, and other parameters.

- **Accessing a Cookie**: Once a cookie is set, you can access its value using the $_COOKIE superglobal array.

- **Deleting a Cookie**: To delete a cookie, you set its expiration time to a point in the past.

**Example: Remembering a User's Preferences Across Sessions**

One common use of cookies is remembering user preferences. For example, a website might store the user's preferred language or theme choice in a cookie so that the website can load with the appropriate settings when they return.

1. **Setting a Cookie**:

php

```
// Set a cookie for 30 days

setcookie("theme", "dark", time() + (30 * 24 * 60 * 60),
"/"); // Expires in 30 days
```

2. **Accessing the Cookie**:

php

```
if (isset($_COOKIE['theme'])) {

    $theme = $_COOKIE['theme'];

    echo "Your preferred theme is: " . $theme;

} else {

    echo "No theme preference found.";

}
```

In this example, a cookie is set to remember the user's theme preference (dark theme). The cookie will expire after 30 days, and on subsequent visits, the website can retrieve the value and display the chosen theme.

**Persistent vs. Session Cookies**

- **Persistent Cookies**: These cookies have a defined expiration time and are stored on the user's device even after the browser is closed.

- **Session Cookies**: These cookies are temporary and are only stored for the duration of the user's session. They are deleted when the user closes the browser.

---

# Securing Sessions and Cookies

While sessions and cookies are powerful tools for handling user data, they can be vulnerable to various security threats. It's important to implement security practices to protect both session data and cookies.

**Session Security Practices**

- **Use Secure Session IDs**: PHP generates a session ID automatically, but it's essential to ensure that the session ID is transmitted securely. You should always use HTTPS to encrypt the session data during transmission.

- **Regenerate Session ID**: After a user successfully logs in, regenerate the session ID to prevent session fixation attacks. This ensures that the attacker cannot reuse the session ID to hijack the session.

```php
```

session_regenerate_id(true);

- **Set Secure and HttpOnly Flags**: When using cookies to store the session ID, set the Secure flag to ensure the cookie is only sent over HTTPS. The HttpOnly flag should be used to prevent client-side JavaScript from accessing the cookie.

```php
```

```php
ini_set('session.cookie_secure', 1);  // Only send cookies over HTTPS

ini_set('session.cookie_httponly', 1); // Prevent access from JavaScript
```

**Cookie Security Practices**

- **Use Secure Cookies**: Always set the Secure flag when storing sensitive data in cookies. This ensures that the cookie is only sent over secure connections (HTTPS).

```php
```

```php
setcookie("user", "JohnDoe", time() + (3600), "/", "", true, true);
```

- **Use HttpOnly Cookies**: Set the HttpOnly flag to prevent cookies from being accessed via JavaScript, protecting against XSS attacks.

- **Cookie Expiration**: Ensure that cookies with sensitive information, such as authentication tokens, expire after a reasonable period and are deleted when no longer needed.

---

In this chapter, we have explored the fundamentals of PHP sessions and cookies, two critical tools for managing user data in dynamic websites. Sessions are useful for temporary data storage and user authentication, while cookies provide a way to store persistent data, such as user preferences.

We have also discussed essential security practices for both sessions and cookies, which help safeguard user data from common attacks such as session hijacking and cookie theft. By following these practices, you can create more secure and robust web applications that provide a seamless and personalized user experience.

As you continue building dynamic websites with PHP, understanding how to work with sessions and cookies will empower you to create more interactive and user-friendly websites, while also keeping user data secure.

# Chapter 7: Implementing User Authentication and Authorization

In this chapter, we will explore the process of implementing user authentication and authorization in PHP. User authentication ensures that users are who they say they are, while authorization determines what actions they can perform once logged in. We will walk through the process of building a secure login system, managing user credentials, and handling user roles and permissions using PHP and MySQL.

## Building a Secure Login System

Creating a secure login system is one of the most important aspects of developing any dynamic website. A secure login system ensures that only authorized users can access sensitive areas of your website. We will use password hashing to ensure that passwords are stored securely and not in plain text.

### Creating the Login Form

The first step in building a login system is to create the user interface for login. This involves a simple HTML form where users can input their credentials (username and password).

html

```
<form action="login.php" method="POST">

    <label for="username">Username:</label>

    <input type="text" name="username"
required><br><br>


    <label for="password">Password:</label>

    <input type="password" name="password"
required><br><br>


    <input type="submit" value="Login">
</form>
```

This form sends the data via the POST method to login.php, where the credentials will be processed.

## Storing User Credentials Securely

When a user registers on your website, you need to store their username and password in the database. However, it is a bad practice to store passwords in plain text. Instead, you should use password hashing to secure user credentials.

PHP offers a simple way to hash passwords using the password_hash() function. This function uses the bcrypt algorithm by default, which is a secure hashing algorithm designed for password hashing.

Here is how you can hash a user's password when they register:

php

```php
<?php
// User registration (registration.php)
if ($_SERVER['REQUEST_METHOD'] == 'POST') {
    $username = $_POST['username'];
    $password = $_POST['password'];


    // Hash the password before storing it in the database
    $hashed_password = password_hash($password, PASSWORD_DEFAULT);


    // Insert into the database (using MySQLi)
    $connection = mysqli_connect("localhost", "username", "password", "database_name");
    $query = "INSERT INTO users (username, password) VALUES ('$username', '$hashed_password')";
    mysqli_query($connection, $query);
```

```php
}
?>
```

In this example, the user's password is hashed using the password_hash() function before being stored in the database. Even if the database is compromised, the actual password remains secure.

**Login Process and Password Verification**

When the user attempts to log in, their input password must be compared against the hashed password stored in the database. To do this, you use the password_verify() function, which checks whether the input password matches the hash stored in the database.

Here's an example of the login processing script:

php

```php
<?php
// Login process (login.php)
if ($_SERVER['REQUEST_METHOD'] == 'POST') {

    $username = $_POST['username'];

    $password = $_POST['password'];


    // Connect to the database

    $connection = mysqli_connect("localhost", "username", "password", "database_name");
```

```php
// Retrieve the stored hash for the username
$query = "SELECT * FROM users WHERE username='$username'";
$result = mysqli_query($connection, $query);
$user = mysqli_fetch_assoc($result);

// Verify the password
if ($user && password_verify($password, $user['password'])) {
    // Successful login
    session_start();
    $_SESSION['user_id'] = $user['id'];
    $_SESSION['username'] = $user['username'];
    header("Location: dashboard.php");
} else {
    // Invalid login
    echo "Invalid username or password.";
}
}
?>
```

In this script:

- The input password is compared to the stored password hash using password_verify().

- If the passwords match, the user is logged in and a session is created to maintain their logged-in state.

---

# User Roles and Permissions

Once the user is authenticated, the next step is to implement authorization. Authorization determines what actions a user can perform based on their role. For example, an admin might have access to additional features like deleting users or managing website settings, while a regular user may only be able to view content.

### Database Design for User Roles

To implement roles and permissions, we need to modify the database schema slightly. We will add a role column to the users table, which will specify the user's role (e.g., admin or regular user).

Here's an example of how you can modify the database structure:

sql

```
CREATE TABLE users (
    id INT AUTO_INCREMENT PRIMARY KEY,
    username VARCHAR(50) NOT NULL,
    password VARCHAR(255) NOT NULL,
    role ENUM('admin', 'user') DEFAULT 'user' -- Role field
```

);

In this schema, the role column determines whether the user is an admin or a regular user. The ENUM type is used to specify the two roles, but you could add more roles if needed.

**Assigning Roles During Registration**

When a new user registers, you can assign a default role of "user." If you have an admin panel, you can allow the administrator to assign the "admin" role to certain users.

php

// Insert a new user with a default 'user' role

$query = "INSERT INTO users (username, password, role) VALUES ('$username', '$hashed_password', 'user')";

**Checking User Roles for Authorization**

Once the user is logged in, you can check their role to determine what they are allowed to do. For example, if the user is an admin, they will have access to certain pages or functionality that regular users do not.

Here's an example of how to check the user's role after they have logged in:

php

<?php

// After login (in dashboard.php)

```php
session_start();

if ($_SESSION['role'] == 'admin') {
    echo "Welcome, Admin!";
    // Provide admin functionalities (e.g., managing users, settings)
} else {
    echo "Welcome, User!";
    // Provide regular user functionalities (e.g., viewing content)
}
?>
```

In this example:

- After a successful login, the $_SESSION['role'] is used to determine if the user is an admin or a regular user.

- If the user is an admin, they have access to additional functionality, such as managing users or settings.

**Admin Panel Example**

In a real-world application, the admin panel might allow the administrator to view and manage users. For example, the admin could see a list of users and be able to delete or promote them.

php

```php
// admin_panel.php
session_start();

if ($_SESSION['role'] != 'admin') {
    echo "Access Denied.";
    exit;
}

// Admin functions (e.g., managing users)
$query = "SELECT * FROM users";
$result = mysqli_query($connection, $query);
while ($row = mysqli_fetch_assoc($result)) {
    echo "Username: " . $row['username'] . "<br>";
}
?>
```

In this example:

- The admin panel first checks if the logged-in user is an admin.

- If the user is not an admin, they are denied access.

- If they are an admin, the list of users is displayed.

# Securing User Authentication and Authorization

While building a login system and handling user roles is essential, security is paramount. Here are some practices to follow for securing user authentication and authorization:

1. **Use HTTPS (SSL/TLS):** Always use HTTPS to encrypt the connection between the user's browser and your server. This ensures that sensitive data, such as passwords and session IDs, are transmitted securely.

2. **Limit Login Attempts:** To prevent brute-force attacks, limit the number of failed login attempts and implement CAPTCHA or other methods to verify that the user is human.

3. **Session Security:** Always regenerate session IDs after login to prevent session fixation. Set session cookies to be secure and use the HttpOnly flag to prevent client-side access.

4. **Role-Based Access Control:** Ensure that users can only access resources and pages for which they have permission. Regular users should not be able to access admin-specific pages unless they have the appropriate role.

5. **Sanitize User Input:** Ensure that all user input, such as usernames and passwords, is sanitized and validated to prevent SQL injection and other types of attacks.

In this chapter, we have covered the process of implementing user authentication and authorization in PHP. By building a secure login system, storing passwords securely with hashing, and managing user roles and permissions, you can ensure that only authorized users have access to specific parts of your website.

We also discussed key security practices, such as using HTTPS, limiting login attempts, and protecting sessions and cookies. By following these best practices, you can build a robust and secure authentication system that keeps your users' data safe while providing personalized experiences based on user roles.

# Chapter 8: Interacting with Dynamic Content

In this chapter, we will dive into how to interact with dynamic content using PHP and MySQL. By understanding the basics of CRUD (Create, Read, Update, Delete) operations, you'll be able to create and manage dynamic data within your web applications. We will also look at how to fetch, display, and interact with this dynamic data, focusing on real-world examples such as managing blog posts, pagination, and sorting.

---

## CRUD Operations (Create, Read, Update, Delete)

CRUD stands for **Create**, **Read**, **Update**, and **Delete**—the four basic operations for managing data. These operations form the backbone of many web applications, such as blogs, e-commerce sites, and social platforms.

### 1. Create (Insert Data into Database)

Creating data is often the first step when interacting with a dynamic website. For example, when a user submits a form to create a new blog post, the data is saved into a MySQL database.

Here's a simplified form for creating a blog post:

html

```html
<form action="create_post.php" method="POST">
    <label for="title">Title:</label>
    <input type="text" name="title" required><br><br>

    <label for="content">Content:</label>
    <textarea name="content" required></textarea><br><br>

    <input type="submit" value="Create Post">
</form>
```

When the form is submitted, the data will be sent to a PHP script (in this case, create_post.php) that inserts the data into a MySQL database.

## PHP Code for Creating Data (Insert into MySQL)

In the create_post.php file, you will handle the form data and insert it into the database using a simple SQL INSERT statement:

php

```php
<?php
// Create new blog post (create_post.php)
```

```php
if ($_SERVER['REQUEST_METHOD'] == 'POST') {

    $title = $_POST['title'];

    $content = $_POST['content'];


    // Connect to the database

    $connection = mysqli_connect("localhost", "username",
"password", "database_name");


    // Escape special characters to prevent SQL injection

    $title = mysqli_real_escape_string($connection, $title);

    $content = mysqli_real_escape_string($connection,
$content);


    // Insert data into the database

    $query = "INSERT INTO posts (title, content) VALUES
('$title', '$content')";


    if (mysqli_query($connection, $query)) {

        echo "Post created successfully!";

    } else {

        echo "Error: " . mysqli_error($connection);

    }
```

```php
mysqli_close($connection);

}
?>
```

In this example:

- The form data is sanitized using mysqli_real_escape_string() to prevent SQL injection.

- A SQL INSERT statement adds the blog post to the posts table in the database.

## 2. Read (Fetch Data from Database)

Reading or retrieving data is a common operation, whether it's displaying posts, users, or products. To fetch data from MySQL, you will use a SELECT query.

Here's an example of fetching and displaying all blog posts:

php

```php
<?php
// Display all blog posts (index.php)

$connection = mysqli_connect("localhost", "username", "password", "database_name");


$query = "SELECT * FROM posts";

$result = mysqli_query($connection, $query);
```

```php
while ($row = mysqli_fetch_assoc($result)) {

    echo "<h2>" . htmlspecialchars($row['title']) . "</h2>";

    echo "<p>" . nl2br(htmlspecialchars($row['content'])) . "</p>";

}


mysqli_close($connection);
?>
```

In this example:

- The SELECT * FROM posts query retrieves all blog posts from the database.

- The htmlspecialchars() function is used to prevent XSS (Cross-site Scripting) attacks by encoding special characters.

- The nl2br() function is used to convert newline characters into <br> tags for proper formatting.


## 3. Update (Modify Existing Data)

Updating data is essential when you want to edit or change existing records, such as updating a blog post's title or content. For this, you will need to fetch the existing data first, allow the user to modify it, and then update it in the database.

### Step 1: Display Existing Post for Editing

php

```php
<?php
// Edit an existing post (edit_post.php)
$post_id = $_GET['id']; // Get post ID from query parameter

$connection = mysqli_connect("localhost", "username", "password", "database_name");

$query = "SELECT * FROM posts WHERE id = '$post_id'";
$result = mysqli_query($connection, $query);
$post = mysqli_fetch_assoc($result);

mysqli_close($connection);
?>

<form action="edit_post.php?id=<?php echo $post['id']; ?>" method="POST">
    <label for="title">Title:</label>
    <input type="text" name="title" value="<?php echo htmlspecialchars($post['title']); ?>" required><br><br>
```

```html
<label for="content">Content:</label>

<textarea name="content" required><?php echo
htmlspecialchars($post['content']); ?></textarea><br><br>

<input type="submit" value="Update Post">
</form>
```

In this code:

- The post's id is passed as a query parameter (?id=123).

- We retrieve the post from the database using a SELECT query and prepopulate the form with the existing data.

**Step 2: Update the Post in the Database**

php

```php
<?php
// Process the updated post (edit_post.php)
if ($_SERVER['REQUEST_METHOD'] == 'POST') {
    $post_id = $_GET['id'];
    $title = $_POST['title'];
    $content = $_POST['content'];

    // Connect to the database
```

```php
$connection = mysqli_connect("localhost", "username", "password", "database_name");

// Escape special characters to prevent SQL injection
$title = mysqli_real_escape_string($connection, $title);
$content = mysqli_real_escape_string($connection, $content);

// Update the post in the database
$query = "UPDATE posts SET title = '$title', content = '$content' WHERE id = '$post_id'";

if (mysqli_query($connection, $query)) {
    echo "Post updated successfully!";
} else {
    echo "Error: " . mysqli_error($connection);
}

mysqli_close($connection);
}
?>
```

In this script:

- The post ID is obtained from the URL parameter ($_GET['id']).

- A SQL UPDATE statement is used to modify the post's title and content in the database.

### 4. Delete (Remove Data from Database)

Deleting data is just as important as creating or updating it. If a user wants to delete a blog post, we can remove it from the database using the DELETE SQL statement.

php

```php
<?php
// Delete a post (delete_post.php)
if (isset($_GET['id'])) {
    $post_id = $_GET['id'];


    // Connect to the database
    $connection = mysqli_connect("localhost", "username", "password", "database_name");


    // Delete the post from the database
    $query = "DELETE FROM posts WHERE id = '$post_id'";


    if (mysqli_query($connection, $query)) {
```

```
    echo "Post deleted successfully!";

} else {

    echo "Error: " . mysqli_error($connection);

}


    mysqli_close($connection);

}

?>
```

In this script:

- The post ID to delete is passed via the URL ($_GET['id']).

- A SQL DELETE statement is executed to remove the post from the posts table.

---

# Displaying Dynamic Content with PHP

Now that we've covered the basic CRUD operations, let's discuss how to display dynamic content based on user interaction. This could involve pagination, sorting, or filtering data to enhance the user experience.

### Example 1: Pagination

Pagination is useful for breaking up large amounts of content into manageable chunks. For example, if you have many blog posts, displaying them all on one page can overwhelm the user. Instead, you can break the posts into pages.

Here's how you can implement pagination in PHP:

php

```php
<?php
// Pagination (index.php)
$connection = mysqli_connect("localhost", "username", "password", "database_name");

$posts_per_page = 5; // Number of posts to display per page
$current_page = isset($_GET['page']) ? $_GET['page'] : 1;
$offset = ($current_page - 1) * $posts_per_page;

$query = "SELECT * FROM posts LIMIT $offset, $posts_per_page";
$result = mysqli_query($connection, $query);

while ($row = mysqli_fetch_assoc($result)) {
    echo "<h2>" . htmlspecialchars($row['title']) . "</h2>";
    echo "<p>" . nl2br(htmlspecialchars($row['content'])) . "</p>";
}
```

```php
$total_posts_query = "SELECT COUNT(*) AS total
FROM posts";

$total_posts_result = mysqli_query($connection,
$total_posts_query);

$total_posts =
mysqli_fetch_assoc($total_posts_result)['total'];


$total_pages = ceil($total_posts / $posts_per_page);


for ($page = 1; $page <= $total_pages; $page++) {
    echo "<a href='index.php?page=$page'>$page</a> ";
}


mysqli_close($connection);
?>
```

In this example:

- The LIMIT clause in the SQL query is used to fetch a subset of posts for the current page.

- The total number of posts is calculated, and the total number of pages is determined by dividing the total number of posts by the number of posts per page.

- Pagination links are generated dynamically based on the total number of pages.

**Example 2: Sorting**

Another way to interact with dynamic content is by sorting it. For example, you might want to sort blog posts by their title or publication date.

php

```php
<?php
// Sorting (index.php)

$sort_order = isset($_GET['sort']) ? $_GET['sort'] : 'ASC';
// Default sort order is ascending

$next_sort_order = $sort_order == 'ASC' ? 'DESC' : 'ASC';


$connection = mysqli_connect("localhost", "username", "password", "database_name");


$query = "SELECT * FROM posts ORDER BY title $sort_order";

$result = mysqli_query($connection, $query);


echo "<a href='index.php?sort=$next_sort_order'>Sort by Title</a>";


while ($row = mysqli_fetch_assoc($result)) {
    echo "<h2>" . htmlspecialchars($row['title']) . "</h2>";
```

```
echo "<p>" . nl2br(htmlspecialchars($row['content'])) .
"</p>";

}


mysqli_close($connection);

?>
```

In this example:

- A query parameter sort is used to determine the sort order.

- Clicking the "Sort by Title" link toggles between ascending and descending order.

---

In this chapter, we explored how to interact with dynamic content using PHP and MySQL. We discussed the four basic CRUD operations (Create, Read, Update, and Delete) and provided real-world examples like managing blog posts. Additionally, we looked at ways to display dynamic content with features such as pagination and sorting to improve user interaction.

By mastering these techniques, you will be able to create full-fledged web applications that manage dynamic data efficiently. Whether it's handling blog posts, products, or user data, these operations form the backbone of many dynamic websites and web applications.

# Chapter 9:
# Introduction to Object-Oriented PHP

In this chapter, we will explore Object-Oriented Programming (OOP) in PHP, a powerful paradigm that improves the scalability, maintainability, and organization of your code. OOP allows developers to model complex systems in a way that mirrors real-world entities and their interactions. With PHP's robust OOP features, you can build scalable and modular applications that are easier to maintain and extend over time.

---

## What is Object-Oriented Programming (OOP)?

Object-Oriented Programming (OOP) is a programming paradigm that organizes code into objects, which are instances of classes. In OOP, data and the functions that operate on that data are encapsulated together into a single unit called a class. A class serves as a blueprint for creating objects, and these objects can then interact with one another by calling methods and sharing properties.

OOP offers a number of key benefits:

- **Encapsulation**: Bundles data and methods that operate on the data within a class, ensuring that internal details are hidden from the outside world (this is called data hiding).

- **Inheritance**: Allows new classes to inherit properties and methods from existing classes, promoting code reuse.

- **Polymorphism**: Enables objects to take many forms, meaning that methods can be implemented in different ways depending on the object context.

- **Abstraction**: Hides complex implementation details while exposing only the necessary interface to the user.

By using OOP in PHP, we can build applications that are more modular, easier to test, and easier to maintain. This is particularly useful when working with large-scale projects.

---

# Explaining OOP Concepts

Let's break down the core concepts of OOP: **Classes**, **Objects**, **Methods**, and **Properties**.

### 1. Classes

A class in OOP is like a blueprint or template for creating objects. It defines the structure and behaviors (methods) that the objects of that class will have. You can think of a class as a recipe, and the object as the dish prepared from that recipe.

Example of a class definition in PHP:

php

```php
class User {
    // Properties (variables)
    public $username;
    public $email;

    // Constructor method (special function to initialize an object)
    public function __construct($username, $email) {
        $this->username = $username;
        $this->email = $email;
    }

    // Methods (functions inside the class)
    public function getUserInfo() {
        return "Username: " . $this->username . ", Email: " . $this->email;
    }
}
```

In this example, we define a class User with:

- **Properties**: $username and $email represent the data that each object will hold.

- **Constructor**: The __construct() method initializes these properties when a new object is created.

- **Method**: The getUserInfo() method returns the user's information.

## 2. Objects

An object is an instance of a class. Once a class is defined, you can create multiple objects based on that class. Each object will have its own set of data (properties), but all objects will share the same behavior (methods).

Example of creating and using an object:

php

```
$user1 = new User("john_doe", "john@example.com");

echo $user1->getUserInfo(); // Outputs: Username: john_doe, Email: john@example.com


$user2 = new User("jane_smith", "jane@example.com");

echo $user2->getUserInfo(); // Outputs: Username: jane_smith, Email: jane@example.com
```

In this example:

- new User() creates a new object based on the User class.

- Each object has its own username and email properties.

## 3. Methods

Methods are functions defined inside a class that operate on the class's properties or perform actions. Methods can take parameters, and can return values.

In our example above, getUserInfo() is a method that returns a string with the user's information.

php

```php
public function updateEmail($newEmail) {

    $this->email = $newEmail;

}
```

This updateEmail() method allows you to modify the email property of the User object.

## 4. Properties

Properties represent the data or state of an object. These are variables that belong to an object, and they define the attributes of the object.

For example, in the User class, $username and $email are properties.

Properties can have different visibility:

- **public**: Can be accessed from anywhere.

- **private**: Can only be accessed within the class.

- **protected**: Can be accessed within the class and by subclasses.

---

# How OOP Makes PHP More Scalable and Maintainable

OOP is especially useful when building large-scale applications, as it promotes:

- **Modularity**: Code is broken down into smaller, reusable components (classes). This makes it easier to maintain, as changes in one part of the code are less likely to affect other parts.

- **Reusability**: Once a class is created, you can reuse it to create many objects, saving time and effort. For example, the User class can be used across multiple pages of your application to manage users.

- **Maintainability**: Since OOP encourages well-defined, modular classes, it's easier to update and modify code without introducing bugs. When you need to make changes, you can often do so by modifying a single class or method rather than digging through the entire codebase.

- **Scalability**: OOP's inheritance and polymorphism features make it easier to extend your application. For instance, you can create a new class that inherits from an existing class, which helps with scaling as your application grows.

---

# Creating a Simple PHP Class

Let's now take a look at an example of creating a class to handle database operations. This class will simplify common database tasks like connecting to the database, inserting records, and fetching data.

**Database Class Example**

php

```php
class Database {
    private $connection;

    // Constructor to initialize the database connection
    public function __construct($host, $username, $password, $dbname) {

        $this->connection = new mysqli($host, $username, $password, $dbname);

        if ($this->connection->connect_error) {
            die("Connection failed: " . $this->connection->connect_error);
        }
    }
}
```

```php
// Method to insert data
public function insert($query) {
    if ($this->connection->query($query) === TRUE) {
        return "New record created successfully";
    } else {
        return "Error: " . $this->connection->error;
    }
}


// Method to fetch data
public function fetch($query) {
    $result = $this->connection->query($query);
    return $result->fetch_assoc();
}


// Destructor to close the database connection
public function __destruct() {
    $this->connection->close();
}
}
```

In this example:

- The Database class encapsulates all database-related logic.

- The insert() method performs an SQL INSERT query.

- The fetch() method retrieves data using an SQL SELECT query.

- The __construct() and __destruct() methods manage the database connection.

**Using the Database Class**

php

```php
// Example of creating a new Database object
$db = new Database("localhost", "username", "password", "database_name");


// Inserting a new user
$query = "INSERT INTO users (username, email) VALUES ('john_doe', 'john@example.com')";
echo $db->insert($query);


// Fetching user data
$query = "SELECT * FROM users WHERE username = 'john_doe'";
$user = $db->fetch($query);
```

echo $user['email'];

In this example:

- The Database class is instantiated and used to insert and fetch data from the database.

---

# OOP Principles in Practice: Real-World Example of User Management

Now, let's use OOP to implement user management in PHP. We will define classes for managing users, including methods for registering users, logging in, and checking if a user exists.

**User Management Class Example**

php

```php
class UserManager {
    private $db;

    public function __construct(Database $db) {
        $this->db = $db;
    }
```

```php
public function registerUser($username, $email,
$password) {

    $passwordHash = password_hash($password,
PASSWORD_DEFAULT); // Secure password hashing

    $query = "INSERT INTO users (username, email,
password) VALUES ('$username', '$email',
'$passwordHash')";

    return $this->db->insert($query);

}


public function loginUser($username, $password) {

    $query = "SELECT * FROM users WHERE username
= '$username'";

    $user = $this->db->fetch($query);


    if ($user && password_verify($password,
$user['password'])) {

        return "Login successful!";

    } else {

        return "Invalid username or password.";

    }

}

}
```

In this example:

- The UserManager class handles user-related operations like registration and login.

- Passwords are securely hashed using PHP's password_hash() and verified with password_verify().

**Using the UserManager Class**

php

```php
// Example of using the UserManager class
$db = new Database("localhost", "username", "password", "database_name");

$userManager = new UserManager($db);


// Register a new user
echo $userManager->registerUser("john_doe", "john@example.com", "securepassword");


// Log in with the existing user
echo $userManager->loginUser("john_doe", "securepassword");
```

In this example:

- The UserManager class is used to register and log in users, abstracting the database logic into reusable methods.

Object-Oriented Programming (OOP) in PHP is a powerful way to organize and manage your code. It promotes modularity, reusability, and maintainability, making your applications easier to scale and update. By using OOP concepts such as classes, objects, methods, and properties, you can build cleaner and more efficient PHP applications. In this chapter, we demonstrated how to create a simple PHP class for database operations and applied OOP principles to build a user management system. Mastering OOP in PHP will greatly improve your ability to develop large-scale, real-world web applications.

# Chapter 10: Advanced MySQL Queries

In this chapter, we will dive into advanced MySQL queries. As your applications grow, so does the complexity of the data you need to work with. Mastering advanced queries like **JOIN operations**, **GROUP BY**, **HAVING clauses**, and query optimization will make you a more effective PHP and MySQL developer. These concepts are essential for building scalable and efficient dynamic websites that interact with large databases.

## Complex SQL Queries

Complex SQL queries are typically used to handle sophisticated data retrieval tasks, often requiring multiple operations to produce the desired results. The main components of complex queries in MySQL are **joins**, **grouping**, and **filters**. These allow us to manipulate and retrieve data from one or more tables in a single query.

Let's break down some of the key concepts.

### 1. JOIN Operations

A **JOIN** operation is used to combine rows from two or more tables, based on a related column between them. MySQL supports several types of joins: **INNER JOIN, LEFT JOIN, RIGHT JOIN**, and **FULL OUTER JOIN** (though the latter isn't supported directly in MySQL).

- **INNER JOIN**: Returns records that have matching values in both tables.

- **LEFT JOIN**: Returns all records from the left table, along with matching records from the right table. If there's no match, NULL values are returned for columns from the right table.

- **RIGHT JOIN**: Similar to LEFT JOIN but returns all records from the right table.

- **CROSS JOIN**: Returns the Cartesian product of two tables.

### Example 1: INNER JOIN

Consider two tables: users and orders.

- users table:
    - id, name
- orders table:
    - order_id, user_id, amount

To retrieve a list of all users and their corresponding order details, you could use an INNER JOIN to combine these tables:

sql

```sql
SELECT users.name, orders.order_id, orders.amount

FROM users

INNER JOIN orders ON users.id = orders.user_id;
```

This query will return a list of users who have placed orders, along with their order IDs and amounts. The join happens on the user_id column from orders and the id column from users.

### Example 2: LEFT JOIN

Now, let's say we want to get a list of all users, including those who haven't placed any orders. In this case, we can use a **LEFT JOIN**:

sql

```sql
SELECT users.name, orders.order_id, orders.amount

FROM users

LEFT JOIN orders ON users.id = orders.user_id;
```

In this case, users without any orders will still be included in the result, but the order_id and amount columns will contain NULL values.

---

## 2. GROUP BY Clause

The **GROUP BY** clause is used to group rows that have the same values in specified columns into summary rows, like "total" or "average". This is often used with aggregate functions such as COUNT(), SUM(), AVG(), MIN(), and MAX() to provide statistical insights into the data.

**Example: Counting Orders per User**

Let's say we want to count how many orders each user has placed:

sql

```
SELECT users.name, COUNT(orders.order_id) AS order_count
FROM users
LEFT JOIN orders ON users.id = orders.user_id
GROUP BY users.name;
```

In this query:

- We use the COUNT() function to count the number of orders for each user.

- The GROUP BY clause groups the result by the name column from the users table.

**Example: Summing Order Amounts**

If we want to find the total amount spent by each user, we can use the SUM() function:

sql

```
SELECT users.name, SUM(orders.amount) AS total_spent
FROM users
INNER JOIN orders ON users.id = orders.user_id
```

GROUP BY users.name;

This query returns the total amount spent by each user based on the amount column in the orders table.

---

### 3. HAVING Clause

The **HAVING** clause is used to filter the results of a GROUP BY query. Unlike the WHERE clause, which filters rows before grouping, HAVING filters rows after the grouping is complete. This makes it especially useful when applying aggregate functions.

### Example: Filtering Groups with HAVING

Suppose we want to find users who have placed more than 5 orders. We can use the HAVING clause to filter the groups after counting:

sql

```
SELECT users.name, COUNT(orders.order_id) AS order_count

FROM users

INNER JOIN orders ON users.id = orders.user_id

GROUP BY users.name

HAVING order_count > 5;
```

This query returns a list of users who have placed more than 5 orders. The HAVING clause filters out users who have placed 5 or fewer orders.

# Real-World Examples: Creating Reports and Querying Data from Multiple Tables

Let's look at some practical scenarios where these advanced MySQL queries come into play.

## 1. Generating Sales Reports

A common task in e-commerce websites is to generate sales reports. You might want to see the total sales for each product over a specific time period. Suppose you have two tables: products and sales.

- products table:
    - id, name
- sales table:
    - sale_id, product_id, quantity, sale_date

We can write a query that uses JOIN, GROUP BY, and SUM() to calculate the total sales per product:

sql

```
SELECT products.name, SUM(sales.quantity) AS total_sales

FROM products

INNER JOIN sales ON products.id = sales.product_id
```

WHERE sales.sale_date BETWEEN '2023-01-01' AND '2023-12-31'

GROUP BY products.name;

This query will return the total quantity sold for each product in 2023, joining the products and sales tables.

## 2. Fetching Recent Orders with Customer Information

Another common scenario is displaying recent orders along with customer information for a dashboard. Suppose you have the following tables:

- customers table:
  - id, name, email
- orders table:
  - order_id, customer_id, order_date, total_amount

You can join the customers and orders tables to retrieve the most recent orders and customer details:

sql

```
SELECT customers.name, customers.email,
orders.order_id, orders.order_date, orders.total_amount

FROM orders

INNER JOIN customers ON orders.customer_id =
customers.id

ORDER BY orders.order_date DESC

LIMIT 10;
```

This query will return the 10 most recent orders, along with the customer's name and email.

---

# Optimizing SQL Queries

As your database grows, performance becomes critical. Inefficient queries can lead to slow response times, especially when dealing with large datasets. Here are some strategies for optimizing your MySQL queries.

### 1. Using Indexes

Indexes are special data structures that improve query performance by allowing MySQL to find rows faster. For example, if you frequently query a table by email, it's beneficial to create an index on the email column.

sql

```sql
CREATE INDEX email_index ON users(email);
```

Indexes speed up read operations, but they come with a cost: they slow down write operations (inserts, updates, deletes) because MySQL has to update the index as well. Therefore, it's important to create indexes on frequently queried columns, but avoid over-indexing your tables.

### 2. Avoiding the N+1 Problem

The **N+1 problem** occurs when your application performs one query to retrieve a list of items, and then it performs additional queries for each item in the list. This results in a large number of queries, leading to performance issues.

For example, imagine fetching all users and then querying each user's orders in a loop. Instead, you can join the users and orders tables in a single query to retrieve the data at once.

### 3. Query Caching

MySQL has a query cache that stores the results of frequently run queries. If the same query is executed again, MySQL can return the cached result instead of executing the query again. To take advantage of query caching, ensure your queries are written in a way that allows MySQL to cache them effectively.

### 4. Optimizing SELECT Queries

When retrieving data, always select only the columns you need. For example, instead of using:

sql

```sql
SELECT * FROM users;
```

You should specify only the necessary columns:

sql

```sql
SELECT id, name FROM users;
```

This reduces the amount of data MySQL has to process and transfer.

**5. EXPLAIN for Query Analysis**

The EXPLAIN keyword can be used to analyze how MySQL executes a query. It provides valuable insight into how MySQL plans to retrieve data, such as whether it will use an index or perform a full table scan.

sql

```
EXPLAIN SELECT * FROM users WHERE email =
'john@example.com';
```

The output will tell you how MySQL plans to execute the query, helping you spot inefficiencies.

---

In this chapter, we explored advanced MySQL queries that are essential for handling complex data retrieval tasks. We covered **JOIN operations**, **GROUP BY** and **HAVING clauses**, and the optimization techniques required to keep queries performant as your database grows. These advanced SQL techniques are invaluable for building data-rich dynamic websites, allowing you to create detailed reports, perform sophisticated data analysis, and retrieve data efficiently.

# Chapter 11: Security Best Practices in PHP and MySQL

In web development, security is an essential aspect of creating reliable, scalable, and trustworthy applications. With the increasing number of cyberattacks, it is critical to understand common security risks and how to mitigate them. In this chapter, we will cover common security risks in web development, such as **SQL injection, XSS (Cross-Site Scripting)**, and **CSRF (Cross-Site Request Forgery)**, and we will explore how to secure both PHP code and MySQL databases.

## Common Security Risks in Web Development

Web applications face various security threats that can lead to data breaches, unauthorized access, and other vulnerabilities. Understanding these risks and knowing how to prevent them is crucial for every web developer.

### 1. SQL Injection (SQLi)

**SQL Injection** is one of the most common and dangerous vulnerabilities in web applications. It occurs when an attacker injects malicious SQL code into a query, allowing them to manipulate the query's behavior, execute arbitrary commands, or gain unauthorized access to the database.

For example, consider the following PHP code that retrieves user information based on a user's id:

php

```php
$query = "SELECT * FROM users WHERE id = '$user_id'";

$result = mysqli_query($connection, $query);
```

If the user_id variable is not properly sanitized, an attacker could submit a value like 1 OR 1=1, which would cause the SQL query to always return true, allowing unauthorized access to the database.

## How to Prevent SQL Injection:

- **Use Prepared Statements**: Prepared statements with bound parameters ensure that user inputs are treated as data, not executable code.

- **Use Parameterized Queries**: Instead of embedding variables directly in the query string, use parameterized queries where the variables are treated as separate values, and the database engine handles the escaping of data.

php

```php
$stmt = $mysqli->prepare("SELECT * FROM users
WHERE id = ?");

$stmt->bind_param("i", $user_id);  // 'i' for integer

$stmt->execute();
```

By using prepared statements, the SQL query is compiled before any data is inserted, ensuring that user inputs are treated as values, not executable code.

## 2. Cross-Site Scripting (XSS)

**Cross-Site Scripting (XSS)** is a vulnerability that allows attackers to inject malicious scripts into web pages that are viewed by other users. The malicious scripts can be used to steal cookies, hijack sessions, or perform other harmful actions.

There are three types of XSS attacks:

- **Stored XSS**: The malicious script is permanently stored in the server (e.g., in a database) and is served to users who access the affected page.

- **Reflected XSS**: The malicious script is reflected from the server in response to an attacker's request (e.g., via a URL query parameter).

- **DOM-based XSS**: The vulnerability exists within the client-side code, where the JavaScript running in the browser can be manipulated by the attacker.

For example, consider the following code that outputs user-submitted data without proper sanitization:

php

```php
echo "Welcome, " . $_GET['username'];
```

If an attacker submits the input
<script>alert('Hacked!');</script>, the script will execute
when the page is loaded, alerting the attacker that their
script has been injected successfully.

**How to Prevent XSS:**

- **Escape User Input**: Always escape special
  characters in user inputs when displaying them in
  HTML. In PHP, the htmlspecialchars() function can
  be used to convert special characters into HTML
  entities.

php

```php
echo "Welcome, " . htmlspecialchars($_GET['username']);
```

- **Use Content Security Policy (CSP)**: A **CSP** is a
  browser feature that helps mitigate XSS by
  restricting the sources of content that can be loaded
  into a web page. By setting a proper CSP, you can
  limit where scripts can come from, reducing the
  chances of XSS attacks.

- **Sanitize HTML Input**: For forms that allow
  HTML content, consider using libraries like
  HTMLPurifier to sanitize input and remove any
  harmful scripts.

### 3. Cross-Site Request Forgery (CSRF)

**Cross-Site Request Forgery (CSRF)** is an attack where an
attacker tricks a user into performing an action they did not
intend to do. For example, if a user is logged into a banking

website, an attacker can craft a malicious link or form that, when clicked by the user, transfers money from the victim's account to the attacker's account.

**How CSRF Works:**

- An attacker embeds a request to a website in a malicious email, forum post, or link. When the user is logged into the website, clicking on this link triggers an unwanted action.

**How to Prevent CSRF:**

- **Use Anti-CSRF Tokens**: An anti-CSRF token is a unique token added to each form submitted by the user. When the form is submitted, the server checks whether the token matches the one stored in the session. If they don't match, the request is rejected.

php

```php
// Create a token and store it in the session
$_SESSION['csrf_token'] = bin2hex(random_bytes(32));
```

```php
// Add token to the form
echo '<input type="hidden" name="csrf_token" value="' . $_SESSION['csrf_token'] . '">';
```

- **Check the Referer Header**: The Referer header is a part of the HTTP request that specifies the page from which the request originated. If the referer does not match the domain of your website, reject the request.

# Securing PHP Code

Securing your PHP code is an essential part of building secure web applications. PHP provides several built-in functions and techniques to help prevent common security vulnerabilities.

## 1. Input Validation

**Input validation** is the process of ensuring that the data entered by the user is in the expected format. It's critical to validate all user inputs, including data from forms, URLs, and cookies. Never trust user input.

**Example of Email Validation:**

php

```php
if (filter_var($_POST['email'],
FILTER_VALIDATE_EMAIL)) {

    echo "Valid email address.";

} else {

    echo "Invalid email address.";

}
```

Always validate inputs according to the expected data type, length, format, and range.

## 2. Parameterized Queries and Prepared Statements

As mentioned earlier, using parameterized queries and prepared statements helps to prevent SQL injection attacks by separating user input from the SQL query.

- **MySQLi Example**:

php

```
$stmt = $mysqli->prepare("SELECT * FROM users WHERE username = ?");

$stmt->bind_param("s", $username);

$stmt->execute();
```

- **PDO Example**:

php

```
$stmt = $pdo->prepare("SELECT * FROM users WHERE username = :username");

$stmt->execute(['username' => $username]);
```

Both approaches ensure that user data is handled as parameters, preventing attackers from injecting malicious SQL code.

### 3. Using Password Hashing

Never store passwords in plain text. PHP offers a built-in function password_hash() to securely hash passwords, and password_verify() to check if a user-entered password matches the stored hash.

**Example**:

php

```
$hashed_password = password_hash($password,
PASSWORD_DEFAULT);
```

// Store $hashed_password in the database

When verifying the password:

php

```
if (password_verify($password, $hashed_password)) {
    echo "Password is correct!";
} else {
    echo "Incorrect password.";
}
```

# Securing MySQL Databases

Securing your MySQL database is just as important as securing your PHP code. A compromised database can expose sensitive information, leading to data breaches and loss of trust.

## 1. User Privileges

MySQL allows you to define privileges for users to control what actions they can perform on your database. It's important to follow the principle of **least privilege** by giving users only the minimum permissions required to perform their tasks.

For example, if a user only needs to read from a table, do not give them write or delete permissions:

sql

```
GRANT SELECT ON my_database.my_table TO
'my_user'@'localhost';
```

## 2. Regular Backups

Regular backups of your database are essential for data recovery in case of an attack, hardware failure, or other disasters. Make sure to schedule regular backups and store them securely (e.g., offsite or in a cloud backup service).

## 3. Encryption

Sensitive data, such as user passwords and financial information, should always be stored in an encrypted format. MySQL provides built-in functions like AES_ENCRYPT() and AES_DECRYPT() for encrypting data.

sql

```
SELECT AES_ENCRYPT('Sensitive Data',
'encryption_key');
```

For PHP, consider using the openssl library to encrypt and decrypt data at the application level.

---

Security should be a top priority in every stage of web development. In this chapter, we covered the essential security risks in web development, including **SQL injection, XSS**, and **CSRF**, and outlined best practices for mitigating these risks. We also discussed securing PHP code through **input validation, parameterized queries, password hashing**, and **session management**. On the database side, we explored **user privileges, backups**, and **encryption** techniques to ensure your MySQL database remains secure.

# Chapter 12: Building a Simple Content Management System (CMS)

In the world of web development, creating and managing dynamic content is one of the most essential requirements. A **Content Management System (CMS)** is a tool that allows users to create, manage, and modify content on a website without requiring specialized technical knowledge. CMS platforms have become a staple in the web development industry, providing flexibility, scalability, and ease of use. In this chapter, we will walk through the process of building a simple CMS using PHP and MySQL, starting with the basics and gradually adding more sophisticated features. We'll also illustrate how a CMS can make managing dynamic content both straightforward and secure.

---

## What is a CMS?

A **Content Management System (CMS)** is software that helps users create and manage digital content. At its core, a CMS allows website owners, administrators, and even non-technical users to update content on their websites without needing to write code or understand the underlying infrastructure.

In the context of web development, a CMS typically allows users to:

- **Add new content** (e.g., articles, blog posts, product pages)

- **Edit existing content**

- **Delete content**

- **Organize content** using categories, tags, or metadata

- **Manage multimedia content** (images, videos, etc.)

- **Manage users and roles**, such as administrators, editors, and authors

While CMS platforms like **WordPress**, **Drupal**, and **Joomla** are widely known, in this chapter, we will focus on creating a **simple CMS** from scratch using PHP and MySQL. This will give you a better understanding of how these systems work and allow you to customize the CMS for specific project needs.

---

# The Need for Dynamic, Editable Websites

Before content management systems became widespread, updating a website meant editing the HTML, CSS, and JavaScript directly. If a website had hundreds or thousands of pages, managing and updating it could quickly become overwhelming. Without a CMS, website updates were often time-consuming and error-prone, requiring technical expertise or reliance on a developer.

With a dynamic, editable CMS, websites can:

- **Easily Update Content**: Non-technical users can update the website's content (such as articles, product listings, etc.) without needing to know how to code.

- **Improve Collaboration**: Multiple users with different roles (such as writers, editors, or administrators) can work on content creation simultaneously.

- **Enhance Site Scalability**: As the website grows, the CMS can help organize content in a way that is easy to manage and navigate.

---

# Overview of a Simple CMS with PHP and MySQL

A simple CMS typically includes the following basic functionality:

1. **Admin Panel**: An interface where the admin (or authorized user) can log in to add, edit, or delete content.

2. **Content Storage**: A database that stores the content, user information, and any other necessary data.

3. **Dynamic Pages**: Front-end pages that display the content stored in the database.

Let's break down the key components of our simple CMS:

## 1. Admin Interface

The admin interface is where the user interacts with the CMS. In this interface, admins can:

- **Log in** to the CMS

- **Add new content** (e.g., blog posts)

- **Edit existing content**

- **Delete content**

## 2. Database Structure

For a basic CMS, you would need at least two database tables:

- **Users**: To store the information about users (e.g., admins and editors)

- **Posts**: To store the content of the posts (e.g., title, body, date, and author)

The **Users** table might look something like this:

sql

```
CREATE TABLE users (

    id INT AUTO_INCREMENT PRIMARY KEY,

    username VARCHAR(50) NOT NULL,

    password VARCHAR(255) NOT NULL,
```

role ENUM('admin', 'editor') NOT NULL,

created_at TIMESTAMP DEFAULT CURRENT_TIMESTAMP

);

The **Posts** table could look like this:

sql

```
CREATE TABLE posts (
    id INT AUTO_INCREMENT PRIMARY KEY,
    title VARCHAR(255) NOT NULL,
    body TEXT NOT NULL,
    created_at TIMESTAMP DEFAULT CURRENT_TIMESTAMP,
    updated_at TIMESTAMP DEFAULT CURRENT_TIMESTAMP ON UPDATE CURRENT_TIMESTAMP,
    author_id INT,
    FOREIGN KEY (author_id) REFERENCES users(id)
);
```

This simple database structure allows the CMS to store both user information and content for blog posts.

### 3. Front-End Display

On the front end, your CMS will display content dynamically by fetching data from the MySQL database and rendering it in HTML. This ensures that the content is always up-to-date without the need for manual updates to the website's static files.

---

# Key Features of a CMS

A basic CMS typically includes the following core features. We'll discuss these in detail to give you a solid understanding of how to implement each one:

### 1. Admin Interface

The **admin panel** allows admins and authorized users to log in and manage content. Here's a breakdown of the key components:

- **Login Page**: Allows administrators to log in using their credentials (username and password).

- **Dashboard**: Once logged in, admins can access a dashboard with an overview of the CMS's current state, such as how many posts exist and any recent activity.

- **Content Management**: Admins can create new posts, edit existing ones, and delete content.

### 2. Add/Edit/Delete Content

The key feature of any CMS is content management. Admins should be able to:

- **Create new posts**: By providing a title, body text, and other metadata (e.g., tags or categories).

- **Edit existing posts**: Update content when necessary.

- **Delete posts**: Remove outdated or irrelevant content.

A typical page for adding or editing content might look like this:

html

```
<form action="save_post.php" method="POST">
    <label for="title">Title:</label>
    <input type="text" id="title" name="title" required><br><br>

    <label for="body">Content:</label>
    <textarea id="body" name="body" required></textarea><br><br>

    <input type="submit" value="Save Post">
</form>
```

Upon submission, the data will be sent to the server-side script (in PHP), which will handle storing it in the database.

### 3. Displaying Content on the Front-End

Once content is created or updated via the admin panel, it should be visible on the website's front-end. This can be achieved by dynamically fetching content from the database and displaying it in the HTML page.

Here's an example of how to fetch and display blog posts using PHP:

php

```php
<?php
$query = "SELECT * FROM posts ORDER BY created_at DESC";
$result = mysqli_query($connection, $query);

while ($row = mysqli_fetch_assoc($result)) {
    echo "<h2>" . htmlspecialchars($row['title']) . "</h2>";
    echo "<p>" . nl2br(htmlspecialchars($row['body'])) . "</p>";
}
?>
```

This code fetches all posts from the database, orders them by their creation date, and displays the title and body on the webpage.

# Real-World Example of Building a Basic CMS for a Blog

Let's consider building a simple blog CMS. The blog will allow administrators to:

- Add new blog posts
- Edit existing blog posts
- Delete posts
- Display posts on the website

### Step 1: Setting up the Database

We will first create the two tables: **users** and **posts**. You can do this via PHPMyAdmin or using SQL scripts. For a blog, the **posts** table will store the post's title, body, and author. The **users** table will store login credentials.

### Step 2: Admin Authentication

We need to set up a login system for the admin interface. You will check the credentials against the database and set a session variable to indicate that the user is logged in.

php

```php
session_start();
if ($_SERVER['REQUEST_METHOD'] === 'POST') {
    $username = $_POST['username'];
    $password = $_POST['password'];
```

```php
// Check credentials in the database

$query = "SELECT * FROM users WHERE username = '$username' LIMIT 1";

$result = mysqli_query($connection, $query);

$user = mysqli_fetch_assoc($result);


if (password_verify($password, $user['password'])) {

    $_SESSION['user_id'] = $user['id'];

    $_SESSION['role'] = $user['role'];

    header('Location: dashboard.php');

} else {

    echo "Invalid credentials";

}

}
```

**Step 3: Adding and Editing Posts**

Once logged in, the admin can go to the dashboard to add or edit blog posts. Here's a simple PHP script to handle adding a new post:

php

```php
if ($_SERVER['REQUEST_METHOD'] === 'POST') {

    $title = $_POST['title'];

    $body = $_POST['body'];
```

```php
$author_id = $_SESSION['user_id'];


$query = "INSERT INTO posts (title, body, author_id)
VALUES ('$title', '$body', '$author_id')";

mysqli_query($connection, $query);

header('Location: dashboard.php');

}
```

## Step 4: Displaying Posts

The final step is to display the posts on the front-end. This involves fetching all posts from the database and displaying them dynamically.

php

```php
$query = "SELECT * FROM posts ORDER BY created_at
DESC";

$result = mysqli_query($connection, $query);


while ($row = mysqli_fetch_assoc($result)) {

    echo "<h2>" . htmlspecialchars($row['title']) . "</h2>";

    echo "<p>" . nl2br(htmlspecialchars($row['body'])) .
"</p>";

}
```

Building a simple CMS using PHP and MySQL allows developers to create dynamic, easily manageable websites. By implementing features like an admin interface for managing content, adding user authentication, and displaying content dynamically, you can quickly set up a content-driven website.

The CMS we've discussed in this chapter is quite basic but lays the foundation for more advanced systems. You can expand this system by adding additional features, such as user management, categories, comments, or even multimedia management.

Ultimately, mastering the creation of a CMS gives you a deeper understanding of how dynamic websites are built and maintained, and opens the door for more advanced development opportunities.

# Chapter 13: Introduction to MVC (Model-View-Controller) Architecture

In this chapter, we will explore the **Model-View-Controller (MVC)** architecture—a design pattern widely used in web development for creating scalable and maintainable applications. By using MVC, developers can separate the concerns of an application into three distinct parts: the model, the view, and the controller. This separation improves the maintainability of code, reduces complexity, and helps manage larger projects more effectively.

The goal of this chapter is to help you understand how the MVC design pattern works in a PHP context, how to structure your applications with MVC, and how to implement a small blog system using this architecture.

# What is MVC?

**MVC (Model-View-Controller)** is a design pattern used in software development to separate the concerns of an application into three distinct components:

1. **Model**: Represents the application's data and the business logic. It manages the data, logic, and rules of the application. The model is responsible for retrieving data from the database, processing it, and returning the results.

2. **View**: Represents the user interface and is responsible for displaying the data to the user. It generates the presentation layer by rendering HTML or other output formats based on the model's data.

3. **Controller**: Acts as an intermediary between the model and the view. It handles user input, processes it (often by modifying the model), and updates the view accordingly. The controller typically receives requests from the user, calls appropriate methods in the model, and then loads the appropriate view to display the results.

The key idea behind MVC is to **separate concerns**:

- The **model** manages the data.

- The **view** presents the data.

- The **controller** acts as a bridge that handles the user's input and updates both the model and the view.

By separating these concerns, MVC helps keep the code modular and easier to maintain, scale, and test.

---

# Explanation of the MVC Design Pattern

In a traditional monolithic application, the different components of the application (such as data handling, business logic, and presentation) are often tightly coupled together. This can lead to difficult-to-maintain code as the application grows. MVC solves this problem by decoupling these concerns.

1. **Model**:

   o The **model** represents the underlying data and the logic behind it. It is responsible for interacting with the database and performing CRUD (Create, Read, Update, Delete) operations.

   o In a PHP application, the model is typically a class or set of classes that correspond to the application's data entities (e.g., users, posts, products).

   o The model does not need to know about the view or controller. It simply provides data to the controller and receives commands to update or retrieve data from the database.

2. **View**:

- The **view** is responsible for rendering data and sending it to the user's browser. It only cares about how to present the data to the user.

- Views are typically HTML templates or PHP files that format and display the data provided by the model.

- The view doesn't contain any logic for fetching or processing the data; it simply receives the data from the controller and displays it.

3. **Controller**:

- The **controller** is the central component in MVC. It processes user input, interacts with the model, and decides which view to display.

- When a user submits a request, the controller handles the request by fetching the appropriate data from the model and passing it to the view.

- The controller acts as a middleman that coordinates the flow of data between the view and the model.

# How MVC Separates Concerns in PHP Applications

By using MVC, PHP developers can build applications with cleaner, more modular code. Let's break down how each part of the MVC pattern helps separate concerns in PHP applications:

- **Model (Data Layer)**: This component contains the data structure and logic for interacting with the database. For instance, in a blog application, the model would include classes for handling blog posts, user accounts, and comments. The model would handle database queries, and it could include methods like createPost(), getPosts(), or deletePost(). The model doesn't know how the data is presented to the user.

- **View (Presentation Layer)**: The view only focuses on presenting the data to the user in a readable and interactive format. The view could include HTML, CSS, and JavaScript files, but it won't contain any logic about how data is fetched or stored. Instead, it will simply receive the data from the controller and render it accordingly.

- **Controller (Business Logic)**: The controller processes user input, interacts with the model, and updates the view. When a user submits a form, clicks a button, or navigates to a specific page, the controller determines how to handle the request. It might fetch data from the model and then pass it to the view to display.

This separation makes the application easier to maintain. For example:

- If we need to update the UI, we only need to modify the view, leaving the model and controller intact.

- If we need to modify how the data is fetched (e.g., changing database queries or logic), we only need to adjust the model.

- The controller can be modified to handle new routes or user actions without affecting the view or model.

---

# Building an MVC Application with PHP

Now that we understand the theory behind MVC, let's go through how to build a simple blog application using the MVC pattern in PHP.

### 1. Basic Structure of an MVC App

The structure of an MVC-based PHP application typically looks like this:

bash

```
/my_mvc_app
    /app
        /controllers
            PostController.php
```

/models

    Post.php

/views

    /posts

        index.php

        view.php

    /core

        Controller.php

        Model.php

        View.php

/public

    index.php

/config

    database.php

- **/controllers**: This folder contains the controller classes, which handle user requests and interact with the models.

- **/models**: This folder contains the model classes that represent the data and contain logic for interacting with the database.

- **/views**: This folder contains the HTML templates or PHP files that render the user interface.

- **/core**: Contains base classes for the controller, model, and view. These classes handle common operations like connecting to the database or rendering views.

- **/public**: This is the public directory that contains the index.php file, which serves as the entry point for all requests.

- **/config**: This directory contains configuration files, such as database connection settings.

## 2. Example: Creating a Small Blog Using MVC

Let's walk through creating a simple blog application using the MVC pattern.

### Step 1: Set up the Model

The model represents the data of the blog. Here's an example of the Post.php model class:

php

```php
// /app/models/Post.php

class Post extends Model {

    public $id;

    public $title;

    public $content;

    public $author;


    public function __construct($id = null) {

        parent::__construct();
```

```php
    if ($id) {

        $this->loadPostById($id);

    }

}


public function loadPostById($id) {

    $sql = "SELECT * FROM posts WHERE id = :id";

    $stmt = $this->db->prepare($sql);

    $stmt->bindParam(':id', $id);

    $stmt->execute();

    $post = $stmt->fetch(PDO::FETCH_ASSOC);

    $this->id = $post['id'];

    $this->title = $post['title'];

    $this->content = $post['content'];

    $this->author = $post['author'];

}


public function getAllPosts() {

    $sql = "SELECT * FROM posts ORDER BY created_at DESC";

    $stmt = $this->db->prepare($sql);

    $stmt->execute();
```

```php
    return $stmt->fetchAll(PDO::FETCH_ASSOC);

  }

}
```

This class interacts with the database to fetch blog posts. The getAllPosts() method retrieves all the posts from the posts table.

### Step 2: Set up the Controller

The controller is responsible for handling user input and passing data to the view. Here's an example of the PostController.php controller class:

php

```php
// /app/controllers/PostController.php

class PostController extends Controller {

  public function index() {

    $postModel = new Post();

    $posts = $postModel->getAllPosts();

    $this->view('posts/index', ['posts' => $posts]);

  }


  public function view($id) {

    $postModel = new Post($id);

    $this->view('posts/view', ['post' => $postModel]);
```

```
    }
}
```

The index() method retrieves all blog posts from the model and passes them to the view, while the view() method retrieves a single post by its ID and passes it to the view.

**Step 3: Set up the View**

The view is responsible for displaying the data to the user. Here's an example of the index.php view file that displays all blog posts:

php

```php
// /app/views/posts/index.php

<?php foreach ($posts as $post): ?>

    <h2><?php echo htmlspecialchars($post['title']);
?></h2>

    <p><?php echo
nl2br(htmlspecialchars($post['content'])); ?></p>

    <a href="/post/view/<?php echo $post['id']; ?>">Read
more</a>

<?php endforeach; ?>
```

This view loops through all the posts and displays their titles and content.

---

The MVC design pattern is an essential concept for modern web development. By separating the concerns of an application into models, views, and controllers, MVC helps developers manage large applications more efficiently. In this chapter, we've learned how MVC helps organize PHP applications and how to implement a small blog system using the MVC architecture.

Using MVC enables developers to scale their applications more easily and maintain clean, manageable codebases. The separation of logic (model), presentation (view), and control (controller) makes the application more modular, reusable, and easier to debug.

# Chapter 14: File Uploads and Handling Media

In this chapter, we will explore how to handle file uploads in PHP and work with media files such as images, documents, and other types of files. File uploads are an essential feature for many modern web applications, allowing users to upload profile pictures, documents, or even media content like videos and audio files. We'll also look at best practices for securely managing and displaying media on a website.

By the end of this chapter, you will have a solid understanding of how to handle file uploads in PHP, how to store files on the server, and how to display them on your website.

## Uploading Files with PHP

Handling file uploads in PHP is relatively straightforward. PHP provides the $_FILES superglobal array to manage file uploads, which stores information about the uploaded file such as its name, size, temporary location, and type.

Let's begin by understanding the process of uploading a file:

## 1. File Upload Form (HTML)

To upload a file using PHP, you first need an HTML form that allows users to select a file. The form must include the enctype="multipart/form-data" attribute to indicate that the form will be uploading files.

Here's an example of a simple form that allows users to upload an image file:

html

```
<form action="upload.php" method="POST"
enctype="multipart/form-data">
    <label for="file">Choose a file:</label>
    <input type="file" name="file" id="file" required>
    <button type="submit">Upload</button>
</form>
```

This form lets the user select a file from their device, which will be sent to the server via a POST request to the upload.php script.

## 2. Handling the File Upload in PHP

In the PHP script (upload.php), you can access the uploaded file through the $_FILES superglobal. This array contains various details about the uploaded file, such as the original filename, file size, temporary location, and MIME type.

Here's an example of how to handle a file upload:

php

```php
<?php
// Check if a file was uploaded
if (isset($_FILES['file'])) {
    $file = $_FILES['file'];

    // Get file details
    $fileName = $file['name'];
    $fileTmpName = $file['tmp_name'];
    $fileSize = $file['size'];
    $fileError = $file['error'];

    // Define allowed file types and the upload directory
    $allowed = array('jpg', 'jpeg', 'png', 'gif');
    $fileExt = strtolower(pathinfo($fileName,
PATHINFO_EXTENSION));

    // Check if the file type is allowed
    if (in_array($fileExt, $allowed)) {
        // Check for errors
        if ($fileError === 0) {
            // Define a unique file name to prevent overwriting
existing files
```

```php
        $fileNewName = uniqid('', true) . '.' . $fileExt;

        $fileDestination = 'uploads/' . $fileNewName;


        // Move the file to the upload directory

        if (move_uploaded_file($fileTmpName,
$fileDestination)) {

            echo "File uploaded successfully!";

        } else {

            echo "Error moving file.";

        }

    } else {

        echo "There was an error uploading your file.";

    }

  } else {

    echo "File type not allowed. Please upload a valid
image.";

  }

} else {

  echo "No file uploaded.";

}

?>
```

**Explanation of the Code:**

1. **Checking for file upload**: The isset($_FILES['file']) checks if a file was submitted through the form.

2. **File information**: The $file array contains details like the file name, temporary location on the server, file size, and any errors encountered during the upload process.

3. **File validation**: We validate the file by checking its extension against a list of allowed file types (in this case, image formats like .jpg, .jpeg, .png, and .gif).

4. **Error checking**: We check for any upload errors and display appropriate messages if the file type is invalid or there are issues during the upload.

5. **Moving the file**: Once validated, the file is moved from its temporary location ($fileTmpName) to the desired upload directory (uploads/), where it will be stored with a unique name.

### 3. Displaying Uploaded Files

After uploading a file, you might want to display it on your website. To do this, you can reference the uploaded file using its new location on the server.

For example, to display an image that was just uploaded:

php

```
<img src="uploads/<?php echo $fileNewName; ?>"
alt="Uploaded Image">
```

This will display the uploaded image from the uploads/ directory.

---

# Storing and Displaying Media

Now that you've seen how to upload a file, it's important to discuss the best practices for storing and displaying media on your website. These best practices ensure that your file upload system is secure, organized, and efficient.

### 1. Organizing Uploaded Files

When handling file uploads, it's essential to organize them properly on the server. A flat directory structure may seem simple initially, but as your application grows, it can become difficult to manage large numbers of files.

Here are a few recommendations for organizing uploaded files:

- **Create subdirectories**: Group files by type (e.g., images/, documents/, videos/) or by user (e.g., users/1/, users/2/).

- **Use unique file names**: Use a unique identifier (e.g., uniqid(), or a random string) when storing the file to prevent name collisions.

- **Limit file storage**: Set size limits to avoid users uploading extremely large files. For example, restrict uploads to a few megabytes (MB).

## 2. Storing Files on the Server

When storing files on the server, you must ensure that the server has adequate file permissions to allow file uploads. Typically, the web server needs write permissions for the directory where files are uploaded.

Here's how you can organize files into subdirectories:

php

```php
$uploadDirectory = 'uploads/' . date('Y/m/d') . '/'; // Store in date-based subdirectories


// Check if directory exists, if not, create it
if (!is_dir($uploadDirectory)) {
    mkdir($uploadDirectory, 0777, true); // Create directories recursively
}


$fileDestination = $uploadDirectory . $fileNewName;
```

This example stores files in subdirectories based on the current date, which helps organize the files better.

## 3. Validating and Securing Uploaded Files

File uploads can introduce several security risks, so it's important to validate files and protect your server against malicious file uploads.

- **File type validation**: Always check the file extension and MIME type to ensure only allowed file types (e.g., .jpg, .png, .pdf) are uploaded.

- **Limit file size**: Use the upload_max_filesize and post_max_size directives in your php.ini file to set limits on the maximum file size.

- **Avoid executing uploaded files**: Never allow uploaded files to be executed directly on the server (e.g., by placing them outside the web root or restricting execution permissions).

- **File content validation**: Check the file's content type, especially for images, by using functions like getimagesize() to validate that the file is an actual image.

## 4. Displaying Media Files

Once files are uploaded and stored on the server, they can be displayed or linked to your application. For instance, after uploading an image, you can dynamically display it by referencing its path on the server:

php

```
<img src="uploads/<?php echo $fileNewName; ?>"
alt="Profile Picture">
```

For non-image files (like PDFs), you can create download links:

php

```
<a href="uploads/<?php echo $fileNewName; ?>"
download>Download File</a>
```

For security reasons, it's important to ensure that users can only access files that they are authorized to see. This may involve using authentication or file access controls to ensure files are only accessible to the right users.

---

# Best Practices for Managing Media Files

Here are some best practices for handling media files in your web applications:

1.  **Sanitize File Names**: Always sanitize file names to prevent security risks, such as directory traversal attacks. Use functions like basename() to remove any directory path from the uploaded file's name.

php

```php
$fileName = basename($file['name']);
```

2.  **Limit Upload Types**: Restrict the types of files users can upload based on your application's needs (e.g., only images or PDFs).

3.  **Secure File Access**: If you store sensitive files (e.g., user documents), ensure they are not directly accessible from the web by placing them outside the public directory and serving them through a script that checks the user's permissions.

4. **Regularly Backup Files**: If your application relies heavily on uploaded media, ensure that you have a backup strategy for important files.

5. **Use Content Delivery Networks (CDNs)**: For media-heavy applications, consider offloading file storage and delivery to a CDN. This can improve performance by caching files and serving them closer to the user.

---

Handling file uploads in PHP is a vital feature for many web applications, from user profile pictures to documents and media content. By following best practices for file validation, organization, and security, you can ensure that your application is robust, secure, and efficient when dealing with uploaded files.

In this chapter, you've learned how to create a simple file upload system, how to store and display media files, and how to implement best practices for file management and security. As you continue developing dynamic websites with PHP and MySQL, handling file uploads will become an essential skill in providing rich, user-driven content and interactions.

# Chapter 15: Handling Large-Scale Data and Optimizing Performance

When developing a dynamic website, the performance and scalability of the application are essential for providing a smooth user experience, especially as the application grows and traffic increases. Large-scale websites need to efficiently handle vast amounts of data, serve millions of users, and operate under varying traffic loads. In this chapter, we will explore techniques for optimizing both PHP and MySQL, ensuring your web application can handle large-scale data effectively.

---

## Scalability Challenges in Web Development

Scalability refers to the ability of a website or application to grow and handle increasing traffic and data over time. A scalable website can handle more users, more requests, and more data without degrading performance.

As websites grow in popularity, they face several challenges:

1. **Increased Load**: More users accessing the website results in more requests to the server, leading to higher load times and slower performance.

2. **Database Bottlenecks**: As the database grows in size, executing queries can become slower, especially for large datasets.

3. **Resource Limitations**: Servers may struggle to process an increasing number of requests simultaneously, leading to resource bottlenecks, such as CPU, memory, or bandwidth limitations.

4. **Network Latency**: If users are located in different regions, network latency can become a problem when serving content from a centralized server.

The key to solving these challenges is scalability, which can be achieved through techniques such as caching, optimizing server-side scripts, and improving database performance.

---

# What Makes a Website Scalable?

There are several key factors that contribute to making a website scalable:

### 1. Caching

Caching is one of the most effective ways to reduce load times and optimize the performance of dynamic websites. By storing frequently accessed data in a temporary storage location (the cache), you can reduce the time it takes to generate dynamic content, which often requires querying the database.

There are two main types of caching in web development:

- **Page Caching**: Entire HTML pages are stored in the cache and served directly to users, avoiding the need to regenerate the page for every request. This is particularly useful for static pages or pages that don't change frequently.

- **Data Caching**: Caching specific data or query results that are frequently requested. For example, you might cache the results of a database query or the output of an API call.

Common caching mechanisms include:

- **Memcached**: A high-performance, distributed memory object caching system. Memcached stores frequently requested data in memory, reducing the need to query the database repeatedly.

- **Redis**: A powerful key-value store that supports advanced data structures, ideal for caching frequently accessed data.

- **OPcache**: PHP's built-in opcode cache that stores precompiled PHP code to reduce the overhead of compiling PHP scripts for each request.

## 2. Database Optimization

As the database grows in size, retrieving data can become increasingly slow. To address this, database optimization techniques can be used to speed up query execution.

Common database optimization techniques include:

- **Indexing**: Indexes allow for faster searching and sorting of data. For example, if you frequently query a table by a specific column (e.g., a user's email address), adding an index on that column will make these queries much faster. However, keep in mind that while indexes speed up read operations, they can slow down write operations (inserts, updates, deletes), so use them judiciously.

- **Query Optimization**: Writing efficient SQL queries is key to improving performance. Avoid using SELECT * (which retrieves all columns) and instead specify only the columns you need. Additionally, using JOINs efficiently and avoiding unnecessary subqueries can also optimize performance.

- **Database Sharding**: Sharding involves splitting the database into smaller, more manageable pieces (shards) that can be distributed across multiple servers. Each shard handles a portion of the database, reducing the load on any single server. Sharding is typically used for very large databases where a single server cannot handle the load.

### 3. Load Balancing

Load balancing is the practice of distributing incoming traffic across multiple servers to ensure no single server is overwhelmed. A load balancer sits between the user and the server, forwarding requests to the least busy server, thereby improving overall application performance and availability.

Load balancing can be done at different layers:

- **DNS Load Balancing**: Distributes traffic to different servers based on DNS (Domain Name System) configurations.

- **Hardware Load Balancing**: Uses dedicated hardware devices that distribute traffic across multiple servers.

- **Software Load Balancing**: Uses software-based load balancing algorithms, often integrated with web servers or reverse proxies like Nginx or HAProxy.

### 4. Horizontal Scaling

Horizontal scaling involves adding more servers to handle increased traffic. Unlike vertical scaling (adding more resources, like CPU or RAM, to a single server), horizontal scaling involves distributing the load across multiple servers to handle more requests simultaneously.

Horizontal scaling is essential for handling traffic spikes and ensuring high availability.

---

# Optimizing PHP for Performance

PHP is a server-side scripting language, and the efficiency of PHP scripts can directly affect the performance of a website. Optimizing PHP for performance is critical, especially when handling large amounts of data.

### 1. Reducing Execution Time

One of the simplest ways to optimize PHP performance is to reduce the execution time of scripts. Here are some strategies:

- **Avoid Unnecessary Computation**: Repeatedly performing the same calculations or querying the database multiple times can slow down your application. Store the results of expensive queries or computations in variables or cache them.

- **Optimize Loops and Algorithms**: Efficient algorithms and loop structures can drastically reduce execution time. Avoid nested loops when possible and look for more efficient alternatives.

- **Use Output Buffering**: PHP's output buffering feature can improve performance by storing the output of a script in memory and sending it all at once to the client, rather than sending it in chunks.

php

```php
ob_start(); // Start output buffering


// Code that generates content


ob_end_flush(); // Send the buffered content to the client
```

## 2. Reduce File I/O Operations

Every time PHP reads or writes a file, it takes time, especially if the file is large or the file system is slow. Avoid frequent file reads or writes within PHP scripts.

Instead, use caching mechanisms like Memcached or Redis to store data that is read often.

## 3. Avoid Unnecessary Database Queries

Minimize the number of database queries in PHP. Repeated queries, especially inside loops, can slow down an application. Where possible, try to perform bulk operations (e.g., batch inserts, updates) and fetch all necessary data in one query, rather than multiple queries.

## 4. Enable Opcode Caching

PHP is an interpreted language, meaning that PHP code is compiled into bytecode each time it runs. Enabling opcode caching stores the compiled bytecode in memory, so PHP doesn't have to recompile the script on every request.

This can be done using tools like **OPcache**, which is built into PHP and is enabled by default in newer versions of PHP.

php

```php
// Check if OPcache is enabled
if (function_exists('opcache_get_status')) {
    echo 'Opcode caching is enabled';
}
```

# Scaling MySQL Databases

As a website grows and its database expands, you may face performance bottlenecks when querying large amounts of data. Here are a few techniques to scale MySQL databases effectively:

## 1. Indexing

Indexes are essential for optimizing database queries, especially for large datasets. Indexes speed up the retrieval of data by allowing the database to search and sort more efficiently.

For example, if you often query a users table by email, adding an index on the email column will improve query performance:

sql

```
CREATE INDEX email_index ON users(email);
```

While indexing improves read performance, it comes at the cost of slower write operations (inserts, updates, deletes), so it's important to carefully consider which columns to index.

## 2. Query Optimization

Writing efficient SQL queries is essential for handling large datasets. Avoid unnecessary joins, subqueries, and operations on non-indexed columns. Always use the EXPLAIN statement to analyze your queries and optimize them:

sql

```
EXPLAIN SELECT * FROM users WHERE email =
'user@example.com';
```

This will show the query execution plan, helping you
identify any performance issues.

### 3. Database Sharding

For very large applications, sharding is an effective
technique to distribute the load across multiple servers.
Sharding involves splitting your database into smaller,
more manageable pieces (shards), and storing them on
separate servers.

For example, you could shard a user database based on user
IDs, storing users with IDs between 1 and 1,000,000 on one
server and users with IDs between 1,000,001 and 2,000,000
on another server.

Sharding can significantly reduce the load on a single
database server and improve performance, but it also adds
complexity, so it should be considered for large-scale
applications only.

### 4. Using Read Replicas

For read-heavy applications, MySQL replication allows
you to create read replicas, which can offload read
operations from the primary database server. This setup is
commonly used in conjunction with load balancing to
distribute the read requests among multiple replicas.

---

Scaling a dynamic website to handle large-scale data and
increasing traffic requires careful consideration of both

PHP and MySQL optimization techniques. Caching, database indexing, query optimization, and horizontal scaling are all important strategies to ensure your application can scale effectively.

By optimizing PHP scripts for performance, using caching mechanisms, and employing strategies like database sharding and replication, you can build a website that performs efficiently, even under heavy traffic. This chapter provides the foundational tools and techniques you need to ensure your web application can grow alongside your users, without sacrificing performance.

# Chapter 16: Using PHP Frameworks (Laravel, Symfony)

When building dynamic websites with PHP, developers often choose to use frameworks to streamline the development process. PHP frameworks provide a structured way of writing code, adhering to best practices and offering useful tools and libraries out-of-the-box. Two of the most popular PHP frameworks are **Laravel** and **Symfony**, each of which offers powerful features that help developers build robust, maintainable, and scalable web applications efficiently. In this chapter, we will explore the benefits of using PHP frameworks and dive into the specifics of **Laravel** and **Symfony**.

## Why Use a PHP Framework?

### 1. Speed of Development

A PHP framework accelerates the development process by providing ready-made libraries, components, and tools that you can use out of the box. This reduces the need to write boilerplate code and lets you focus on the unique functionality of your application. A framework speeds up tasks such as routing, form validation, authentication, and database management, making the overall development process much faster.

## 2. Structure and Organization

PHP frameworks impose a clear structure on the application, enforcing a specific architecture that ensures the code is organized and maintainable. The framework provides a standard way to organize files, manage requests, and handle databases, which helps prevent the chaos that often arises from writing custom code without a clear structure.

For instance, both **Laravel** and **Symfony** use the **MVC (Model-View-Controller)** architecture, which separates the application logic into three layers:

- **Model**: Handles data and business logic.

- **View**: Represents the presentation layer, i.e., the user interface.

- **Controller**: Manages the flow of data between the Model and the View.

This separation of concerns makes your application more organized, maintainable, and scalable.

## 3. Security

Frameworks like Laravel and Symfony come with built-in security features to protect your application from common vulnerabilities such as SQL injection, Cross-Site Scripting (XSS), and Cross-Site Request Forgery (CSRF). By using these frameworks, you inherit secure methods for handling user input, sanitizing data, and protecting sessions, which can be challenging to implement manually. This allows developers to focus more on the business logic of the application rather than worrying about security.

**4. Community Support and Ecosystem**

Both Laravel and Symfony have large and active communities that contribute to the framework's development and offer extensive documentation and tutorials. The frameworks also come with a wide range of third-party packages and plugins, which you can integrate into your application to add functionality without having to write custom code.

In addition, both frameworks have robust support for testing, making it easier to write automated tests and ensure that your application functions correctly as it grows and evolves.

---

# Introduction to Laravel

Laravel is a modern PHP framework that has gained immense popularity due to its elegant syntax, powerful features, and developer-friendly tools. It follows the **MVC** pattern and provides a wide array of built-in tools for common tasks such as authentication, routing, database management, and session handling.

**Basic Features of Laravel**

**1. Routing**

Laravel makes routing simple and expressive. Instead of manually defining routes, you can use a clean and intuitive syntax to create routes in the routes/web.php file. Laravel also supports RESTful routing, which is commonly used in APIs.

Example:

php

```php
Route::get('/home', [HomeController::class, 'index']);
```

This simple route will handle GET requests to the /home URL and map them to the index method of the HomeController class.

## 2. Eloquent ORM

Eloquent is Laravel's built-in Object-Relational Mapping (ORM) system, which provides an elegant, fluent interface for interacting with databases. Eloquent allows you to interact with your database tables as if they were objects in PHP, making database operations more intuitive.

Example:

php

```php
$user = User::find(1);  // Find a user by ID

$user->name = 'John Doe';  // Update the user's name

$user->save();  // Save changes to the database
```

Eloquent automatically handles SQL queries behind the scenes, allowing you to focus on the logic rather than the database syntax.

## 3. Blade Templating Engine

Blade is Laravel's templating engine, which allows you to define reusable views and layouts for your application. Blade makes it easy to include dynamic content and create reusable sections of HTML. Blade's syntax is simple and clean, making it easy to work with PHP and HTML together.

Example:

blade

```
@extends('layouts.app')


@section('content')
    <h1>Welcome to Laravel!</h1>
@endsection
```

In this example, the content section is rendered inside a layout defined by layouts.app.

## 4. Authentication

Laravel provides a simple way to implement user authentication, including login, registration, and password reset functionality. Laravel's built-in authentication system is easy to set up and can be customized as needed.

You can use Laravel's artisan commands to quickly generate authentication scaffolding, which includes routes, controllers, and views:

bash

```
php artisan make:auth
```

**Example: Building a Simple Laravel Application**

Let's look at a simple Laravel application that allows users to create and view blog posts. The steps below outline the basic setup:

1. **Create a New Laravel Project**: Run the following command to create a new Laravel application:

bash

```
composer create-project --prefer-dist laravel/laravel blog-app
```

2. **Define Routes**: Open the routes/web.php file and define the routes for the blog:

php

```
Route::get('/', [PostController::class, 'index']);

Route::get('/post/{id}', [PostController::class, 'show']);

Route::post('/post', [PostController::class, 'store']);
```

3. **Create a Controller**: Generate a PostController using the artisan command:

bash

```
php artisan make:controller PostController
```

4. **Create Views**: In the resources/views directory, create Blade templates to display the blog posts and a form to add new posts.

5. **Define Models**: Define an Eloquent model for the Post table:

bash

```
php artisan make:model Post
```

---

# Symfony Overview

Symfony is another powerful and flexible PHP framework used to build large-scale web applications. Unlike Laravel, Symfony is often used for building full-stack applications, but it can also be used as a set of components for more lightweight or custom applications. Symfony is known for its robustness, flexibility, and extensive documentation, making it suitable for enterprise-level applications.

### Symfony Components

Symfony is built around a collection of reusable components that can be used independently of the framework. Some of the most commonly used components include:

- **Routing**: Handles URL routing, mapping URLs to controller actions.

- **Dependency Injection (DI)**: Manages the dependencies between objects and allows for better flexibility and testing.

- **Twig**: A powerful templating engine used for rendering views.

- **Security**: A complete security system for authentication, authorization, and access control.

**Full-Stack Symfony Applications**

Symfony is designed to be modular, meaning you can choose to use just the components you need for your application. However, for full-stack applications, Symfony provides a complete framework with everything you need to build modern web applications, including routing, templating, and security features.

Example of a basic Symfony routing definition:

yaml

```yaml
# config/routes.yaml
homepage:
  path: /
  controller: App\Controller\HomeController::index
```

In Symfony, the routes are typically defined in YAML, XML, or annotations, giving developers flexibility in how they configure their application.

**Building a Symfony Application**

Just like Laravel, Symfony has tools to quickly scaffold basic functionality. You can use the Symfony CLI to create a new project:

bash

symfony new blog-app --full

Once the project is created, you can define routes, create controllers, and build views similar to the Laravel process, but with Symfony's specific conventions and components.

---

Both **Laravel** and **Symfony** offer powerful tools to make web development faster, more efficient, and more secure. Laravel is a great choice for developers who want an easy-to-use, opinionated framework with lots of out-of-the-box features. On the other hand, Symfony provides a more flexible and modular approach, making it suitable for larger applications or for developers who prefer more control over their projects.

By using these frameworks, you can build dynamic websites and web applications more efficiently while adhering to best practices in code structure, security, and scalability. Whether you choose Laravel for its simplicity or Symfony for its flexibility, both frameworks are excellent choices for modern PHP development.

# Chapter 17: Testing and Debugging PHP Applications

Testing and debugging are essential practices in the development of any web application, especially when building dynamic websites with PHP and MySQL. These processes ensure that your website operates reliably, that any issues are quickly identified and fixed, and that new features do not break existing functionality. In this chapter, we'll explore the importance of testing in web development, debugging techniques specific to PHP, and best practices for testing PHP applications through Unit Testing and Test-Driven Development (TDD).

## Importance of Testing in Web Development

In the context of dynamic websites built with PHP and MySQL, testing plays a critical role in ensuring the robustness, stability, and scalability of the application. Web applications are often complex, with interactions between the user interface, the server, the database, and external services. Without comprehensive testing, it's easy for bugs to go unnoticed, leading to security vulnerabilities, performance issues, and user dissatisfaction.

**Why Testing is Crucial**

1. **Reliability**: Testing ensures that the code works as expected in different scenarios. It helps prevent errors that could disrupt the user experience or cause the application to fail entirely.

2. **Regression Testing**: When making changes to the codebase (e.g., adding new features or fixing bugs), tests verify that existing functionality still works correctly and that no new issues have been introduced. This is particularly important in dynamic websites, where the complexity grows over time.

3. **Security**: Many web applications, especially those that involve user input, face security risks such as SQL injection or Cross-Site Scripting (XSS). Tests can help verify that security measures are correctly implemented and that user data is handled securely.

4. **Performance**: Automated testing helps ensure that performance optimizations, such as database query optimizations or PHP script optimizations, do not break existing features or degrade performance.

5. **Code Quality**: Writing tests encourages clean, modular code that's easier to maintain, debug, and extend.

# Debugging Techniques in PHP

Debugging is the process of identifying and fixing errors or "bugs" in the application. In PHP, debugging techniques are essential for quickly finding the root cause of issues, especially in a dynamic website environment where the front end and back end are tightly integrated.

## 1. Using Built-In PHP Error Handling

PHP has a built-in error handling system that can help developers identify issues in their code. By default, PHP generates error messages for syntax errors and runtime issues, but you can customize how errors are reported to get more detailed information.

### Basic Error Reporting

You can enable error reporting in PHP by modifying the php.ini configuration file or by adding the following lines of code in your script:

php

```php
error_reporting(E_ALL);  // Report all errors

ini_set('display_errors', 1);  // Display errors in the browser
```

This setting will help you identify any warnings, notices, and errors that occur during script execution. It's important to disable error display in a production environment to prevent sensitive information from being exposed to users.

## 2. Using Xdebug for PHP Debugging

**Xdebug** is a powerful debugging tool that provides advanced features such as step debugging, stack traces, and profiling. It allows developers to pause execution at specific points (breakpoints), inspect variables, and trace the flow of execution to help identify bugs.

**Setting Up Xdebug**

1. **Install Xdebug**: You can install Xdebug on your local machine using a package manager or by downloading the extension from Xdebug's website.

2. **Configure PHP to Use Xdebug**: After installing Xdebug, you need to configure PHP to use the extension by editing the php.ini file:

ini

```
zend_extension="path/to/xdebug.so"  # Path to the Xdebug extension

xdebug.remote_enable=1  # Enable remote debugging

xdebug.remote_host=localhost  # Localhost for local debugging

xdebug.remote_port=9000  # Default port for debugging
```

3. **Using Xdebug in IDEs**: Most modern IDEs, such as PhpStorm or Visual Studio Code, have built-in support for Xdebug. You can set breakpoints in your code, step through execution, and inspect variables in real-time, making it easier to find and fix issues.

**3. Debugging Tools for Logging**

While Xdebug is great for interactive debugging, logging is another useful debugging technique. PHP's error_log() function allows you to log custom messages to a file, which can help track down issues in production environments where you may not be able to use Xdebug.

Example of logging an error:

php

```
error_log("An error occurred with the user ID: " .
$user_id);
```

This will write the error message to the PHP error log, which can be helpful when troubleshooting issues on live servers.

---

# Unit Testing and Test-Driven Development (TDD)

### 1. Introduction to Unit Testing

Unit testing is the process of testing individual parts (units) of your application to ensure they perform as expected. In PHP, unit testing is typically done using testing frameworks like **PHPUnit**, which allows you to write and automate tests for your code.

### Why Unit Testing Matters

Unit testing allows you to:

- Verify that each component of your application works correctly in isolation.

- Catch bugs early, especially as the codebase grows.

- Improve code maintainability and refactorability by ensuring existing functionality is preserved.

For example, if you are building a dynamic website that allows users to submit comments on blog posts, you could write a unit test to ensure that the comment submission logic correctly stores data in the database.

**Writing a Simple PHPUnit Test**

PHPUnit is a popular testing framework for PHP. It allows you to define test cases using assertions to check if the code produces the expected results.

1. **Install PHPUnit** using Composer:

bash

```
composer require --dev phpunit/phpunit
```

2. **Write a Simple Test Case**:

Create a new file called TestComment.php in your tests directory:

php

```php
<?php
use PHPUnit\Framework\TestCase;
```

```php
class TestComment extends TestCase
{
    public function testCommentSubmission()
    {
        $comment = new Comment();
        $comment->setContent("This is a test comment.");
        $this->assertEquals("This is a test comment.",
$comment->getContent());
    }
}
```

In this simple test case, we are testing the Comment class to ensure that when we set the comment's content, it correctly returns the same content.

3. **Run PHPUnit**:

Run the test from the command line:

bash

vendor/bin/phpunit tests/TestComment.php

If the test passes, you'll see a message confirming that the test was successful. If it fails, PHPUnit will display information about the failure, including the expected and actual results.

## 2. Test-Driven Development (TDD)

Test-Driven Development (TDD) is a software development methodology where you write tests for your application **before** writing the code to implement the functionality. The TDD cycle consists of three steps:

1. **Red**: Write a test for a new feature, but the test will fail because the feature hasn't been implemented yet.

2. **Green**: Write the minimum amount of code needed to pass the test.

3. **Refactor**: Refactor the code to improve its structure while ensuring that the tests still pass.

**Example of TDD Cycle**

Let's say you're adding a feature to calculate the total price of items in a shopping cart.

1. **Write the test**: First, write a test for the cart's getTotalPrice method, expecting it to return the correct total.

2. **Write the code**: Implement the getTotalPrice method so that the test passes.

3. **Refactor the code**: Once the test passes, refactor the code for clarity or efficiency, while ensuring the test still passes.

TDD helps ensure that the code meets the requirements from the start and reduces the likelihood of bugs or feature creep.

---

Testing and debugging are vital aspects of developing dynamic websites with PHP and MySQL. While debugging tools like Xdebug and logging help identify and fix issues, writing unit tests and adopting Test-Driven Development (TDD) can significantly improve the reliability and maintainability of your code.

As web applications grow more complex, the importance of having automated tests in place becomes even more evident. Unit testing helps ensure that your application's individual components behave as expected, while TDD fosters better code design and prevents bugs from being introduced in the first place. By incorporating these testing and debugging techniques into your PHP development workflow, you can build dynamic websites that are not only functional but also reliable, secure, and scalable.

# Chapter 18: Deploying Your PHP and MySQL Website

Building a dynamic website with PHP and MySQL is an exciting and rewarding process. However, once you've developed and thoroughly tested your website, the next crucial step is deploying it to the web, so your users can access it. This chapter will guide you through the process of preparing your PHP and MySQL website for production, deploying it on various hosting platforms, and maintaining and updating the website after it's live. We'll also explore real-world examples and best practices to ensure that your website runs smoothly, efficiently, and securely after deployment.

## Preparing for Production

Before deploying your website to a live server, it's important to prepare it for production. This stage involves optimizing the code, making the website secure, and ensuring it performs well under real-world conditions. Here are some key tasks to consider when preparing your website for production:

### 1. Code Optimization and Minification

When developing your website, you might include extra spaces, comments, or unoptimized code to aid in readability and debugging. However, once your website is ready for production, it's time to clean up and optimize your code to improve performance. Key steps include:

- **Minifying CSS, JavaScript, and HTML**: Minification reduces the size of the code by removing unnecessary characters, comments, and spaces. This improves loading times by decreasing the file size.

    - Use tools like **CSS Minifier**, **UglifyJS**, or **HTMLMinifier** to automatically minify your front-end assets.

- **Compressing Images**: Large image files can slow down your website's loading time. Tools like **TinyPNG** or **ImageOptim** can help reduce image file sizes without compromising quality.

- **Database Optimization**: Clean up and optimize your MySQL database by removing unused data, optimizing tables, and indexing frequently accessed columns to speed up queries.

## 2. Error Reporting and Debugging

During development, you likely used error reporting to debug your website. However, when deploying your site to production, you should disable verbose error reporting to prevent exposing sensitive information to end users. You can do this by modifying your php.ini file or disabling display_errors in your PHP script:

php

```php
ini_set('display_errors', 0);

error_reporting(E_ERROR | E_WARNING | E_PARSE);
```

Instead of displaying errors to users, you should log errors to a file for review. This way, if issues arise, you can trace the problem without compromising user experience.

php

```php
ini_set('log_errors', 1);

ini_set('error_log', '/path/to/error_log');
```

## 3. Security Measures

Security is a top priority when deploying a dynamic website. Here are a few things to consider before going live:

- **SSL/TLS Encryption**: Ensure that your website uses HTTPS by installing an SSL certificate. HTTPS encrypts data transmitted between the server and users, protecting sensitive information such as login credentials and payment data. Platforms like **Let's Encrypt** offer free SSL certificates.

- **Secure Database Connections**: Use prepared statements and parameterized queries in PHP to prevent SQL injection attacks. Ensure that your MySQL database is only accessible to the necessary IP addresses, and use strong authentication methods.

- **Secure File Uploads**: If your website allows users to upload files (such as profile pictures or documents), ensure that you validate the file types, sizes, and file extensions to prevent malicious uploads. Store files in a separate directory and restrict execution permissions.

### 4. Backup and Rollback Plan

Before deploying, ensure you have a solid backup strategy. Back up your database and files, and ensure you can quickly restore the website in case of failure. This is especially important if you're working with a content management system (CMS) or dynamic user-generated content.

---

# Deploying on Shared Hosting, VPS, and Cloud Platforms

There are various hosting options available for deploying PHP and MySQL websites, each offering different levels of control, scalability, and price. The choice of hosting depends on your project's size, budget, and traffic expectations.

### 1. Shared Hosting

Shared hosting is the most affordable hosting option, where your website shares resources with other websites on the same server. Popular shared hosting providers include **Bluehost**, **HostGator**, and **SiteGround**. This option is ideal for smaller websites or personal projects with low traffic.

**Steps to deploy on Shared Hosting**:

1. **Upload Files**: Use FTP (e.g., FileZilla) or the hosting provider's file manager to upload your PHP files to the server's public_html directory.

2. **Set Up MySQL Database**: Most shared hosting providers offer an interface (like **cPanel**) to create and manage databases. Create your MySQL database and import your data using **phpMyAdmin** or command line tools.

3. **Configure Database Connection**: Update the database connection settings in your PHP scripts to match the live database credentials.

4. **Test Your Site**: Once the files are uploaded and the database is connected, test the website by accessing it through the provided domain.

## 2. Virtual Private Server (VPS)

A Virtual Private Server (VPS) provides more control than shared hosting by offering dedicated resources and the ability to install custom software. Providers like **DigitalOcean**, **Linode**, and **Vultr** offer affordable VPS options.

**Steps to deploy on VPS**:

1. **Set Up the Server**: Deploy a VPS instance with your preferred operating system (Linux is most common for PHP websites). You'll typically have to install a web server (Apache or Nginx), PHP, and MySQL manually.

2. **Upload Files**: Use FTP, SFTP, or SCP to transfer your website's files to the VPS.

3. **Install Required Software**:

   o   Install Apache or Nginx (web server).

   o   Install PHP and necessary extensions (e.g., PHP MySQL extension).

   o   Install MySQL or MariaDB (database server).

4. **Configure Database**: Create your database on MySQL, import your database schema, and update your PHP scripts with the correct database credentials.

5. **Secure Your Server**: Harden your VPS by setting up a firewall (e.g., **ufw**), using SSH keys for authentication, and disabling root login.

6. **Configure Domain and SSL**: Set up your domain name to point to your VPS and configure SSL using Let's Encrypt or another SSL provider.

## 3. Cloud Platforms (e.g., DigitalOcean, Heroku, AWS)

Cloud platforms like **DigitalOcean**, **AWS (Amazon Web Services)**, and **Heroku** provide scalable hosting solutions for PHP and MySQL applications. These platforms are more flexible than shared hosting and VPS, as they can easily scale to handle high traffic volumes.

- **DigitalOcean**: Provides scalable droplets (virtual machines), managed databases, and easy-to-use interfaces for deploying PHP and MySQL websites.

- **Heroku**: A platform-as-a-service (PaaS) provider that simplifies the deployment process by handling the infrastructure for you. Heroku supports PHP and

MySQL and allows for automatic scaling based on traffic demands.

- **AWS EC2**: Offers scalable compute capacity on virtual servers. It's ideal for large-scale projects where you need control over every aspect of the server configuration.

**Steps to deploy on Heroku**:

1. **Install Heroku CLI**: Use the Heroku Command Line Interface (CLI) to manage your application.

2. **Deploy the Application**:
   - Initialize a Git repository for your project.
   - Deploy the project using git push heroku master.

3. **Configure the Database**: Use Heroku's Postgres or MySQL add-ons for database management. You can connect to the database using Heroku's environment variables.

4. **Set Up Domain and SSL**: Configure custom domains via the Heroku dashboard and use their automated SSL certificate installation.

---

# Maintenance and Updates

Once your website is live, ongoing maintenance and updates are crucial for keeping it secure, functional, and up-to-date.

### 1. Monitoring and Troubleshooting

Regularly monitor the health and performance of your website. Set up monitoring tools like **UptimeRobot**, **New Relic**, or **Datadog** to track server uptime, page load times, and error rates. If something goes wrong, you can identify issues early and take corrective actions.

### 2. Backups and Disaster Recovery

Ensure that you have an automated backup solution for both the files and databases. This way, in case of an emergency (such as data loss or corruption), you can restore the website quickly. Services like **BackupBuddy** (for WordPress) or **R1Soft** provide backup solutions that integrate seamlessly with PHP websites.

### 3. Updates and Patches

Keep your PHP, MySQL, and all related software up to date. This helps ensure security patches and performance improvements are applied. Additionally, update any third-party libraries or dependencies your website uses, including CMS systems or PHP frameworks.

### 4. Scaling the Website

As your website grows and experiences increased traffic, you may need to scale your hosting resources. On a VPS or cloud platform, you can scale vertically by upgrading the server's resources (e.g., more CPU or RAM) or horizontally by adding additional server instances and using load balancing to distribute traffic evenly.

For MySQL databases, consider using **replication**, **clustering**, or **sharding** to handle larger datasets and improve performance.

Deploying a PHP and MySQL website is an essential phase in bringing your project to life. By following best practices for optimization, security, and scalability, you ensure that your website performs well, remains secure, and is easy to maintain post-launch. Whether you choose shared hosting, VPS, or cloud platforms like DigitalOcean or Heroku, deploying your website requires attention to detail and planning.

Finally, remember that after deployment, continuous maintenance, updates, and monitoring are vital to keeping your website running smoothly as user traffic grows and as new technologies and features emerge. By mastering the deployment process, you are well on your way to becoming a proficient web developer, capable of creating professional, scalable, and reliable websites.

# Conclusion: Next Steps for Mastery in Building Dynamic Websites with PHP and MySQL

Congratulations! You've made it to the end of this journey, learning the essential skills for building dynamic websites using PHP and MySQL. By now, you should have a strong foundation in server-side programming, database management, web security, and application deployment. However, the journey doesn't end here. The world of web development is vast and ever-evolving, and there are always new tools, techniques, and best practices to explore. In this conclusion, we'll provide guidance on how to take the knowledge you've gained and continue to grow as a web developer.

---

## Next Steps for Mastery

The best way to truly master web development is through continuous learning and hands-on practice. Here's how you can continue improving your skills and move from a beginner to an advanced developer:

### 1. Deepen Your Knowledge of PHP and MySQL

While you've covered the fundamentals, both PHP and MySQL are vast technologies with many advanced concepts worth exploring.

- **Advanced PHP Concepts**: Look into advanced topics such as **namespaces, traits, closures,** and **exceptions handling**. Learning more about PHP's **object-oriented programming (OOP)** features, including **design patterns** like **Singleton, Factory,** and **Observer,** can greatly improve the scalability and maintainability of your code.

- **Database Optimization**: Delve deeper into MySQL features like **stored procedures, triggers,** and **views**. Learn about advanced query optimization techniques, including **joins, subqueries,** and the use of **indexes** to speed up queries.

- **SQL Performance Tuning**: As websites grow and traffic increases, the performance of your MySQL database becomes crucial. Understanding how to optimize your database through **caching, sharding,** and **replication** will be key for large-scale applications.

- **Error Handling and Debugging**: Mastering **logging, error handling,** and **debugging tools** (like **Xdebug**) will help you write more reliable and maintainable applications. You'll also need to get comfortable with using a **version control system** (like **Git**) to manage your code and collaborate with others.

**2. Explore Modern Web Technologies and Frameworks**

PHP is an excellent choice for server-side programming, but it's important to stay updated with modern tools and practices that can enhance your productivity and application performance. Here are a few technologies and tools you should consider learning:

- **PHP Frameworks**: Frameworks like **Laravel**, **Symfony**, and **CodeIgniter** streamline web development by providing built-in functionality for common tasks like authentication, routing, and database management. For instance, Laravel's **Eloquent ORM** and **Blade templating engine** offer a more intuitive way of working with PHP.

- **JavaScript Frameworks**: Learn client-side frameworks like **React**, **Vue.js**, or **Angular**. These frameworks allow you to create rich, dynamic front-end applications that can integrate seamlessly with your PHP backend.

- **RESTful APIs**: As modern web development increasingly moves toward API-driven architectures, understanding how to build and consume **RESTful APIs** (using PHP or other technologies) is essential for building scalable, decoupled applications.

- **Version Control and DevOps**: Familiarize yourself with version control systems like **Git** and **GitHub** for collaboration and code management. Learn basic **DevOps** concepts to streamline deployment, continuous integration, and testing.

# Recommended Resources for Continued Learning

To continue growing as a PHP and MySQL developer, it's important to tap into a variety of resources that can offer you deeper insights, best practices, and real-world examples. Here are some excellent resources for advancing your skills:

## Books and Guides

1. **"PHP and MySQL Web Development" by Luke Welling and Laura Thomson**: This book is a great next step if you're looking for in-depth coverage of PHP and MySQL in real-world applications.

2. **"Modern PHP: New Features and Good Practices" by Josh Lockhart**: This book covers modern PHP development practices, including namespaces, dependency injection, and tools for better code organization.

3. **"Learning SQL" by Alan Beaulieu**: A highly recommended book for diving deeper into SQL and MySQL's advanced capabilities.

4. **"Laravel: Up & Running" by Matt Stauffer**: If you're interested in learning Laravel, this book provides an excellent introduction and a guide to building real applications with it.

## Online Courses and Tutorials

1. **Khan Academy Computer Science**: For an interactive and structured approach to learning

computer science concepts, Khan Academy's tutorials are an excellent starting point.

2. **Codecademy**: Offers in-depth courses on PHP, SQL, and web development. It's great for hands-on learning.

3. **Udemy**: Courses like **"The Complete Web Developer Bootcamp"** and **"PHP for Beginners"** are fantastic resources for learning PHP, MySQL, and full-stack web development.

4. **Laracasts**: For PHP and Laravel developers, Laracasts offers a comprehensive video library for mastering PHP frameworks and best practices.

## Forums and Communities

- **Stack Overflow**: A place to get help with specific coding issues and learn from experienced developers.

- **Reddit's r/PHP and r/webdev**: Join the discussion and get advice from web developers at various skill levels.

- **PHP and Laravel Slack Communities**: Connect with other developers and get real-time support on PHP and Laravel development.

## Official Documentation

- **PHP Manual**: The official PHP manual is the most authoritative and detailed source of PHP information. It's essential for understanding functions, libraries, and syntax.

- **MySQL Documentation**: Learn advanced SQL techniques, MySQL configurations, and optimization tips from the official MySQL documentation.

- **Laravel Documentation**: If you're diving into Laravel, the official documentation is well-written and provides a comprehensive guide to the framework.

---

# Encouragement to Keep Practicing with Real-World Projects

At this point, you should feel confident in your ability to build dynamic websites and web applications with PHP and MySQL. However, true mastery comes with continuous practice and experience. Real-world projects provide you with the opportunity to apply the concepts you've learned in a practical context.

### Start Your Own Projects

One of the most effective ways to continue growing as a web developer is by building your own projects. Start with something manageable, like a **blog platform, e-commerce site**, or **personal portfolio**. These projects will allow you to practice:

- Designing and developing database schemas.

- Implementing user authentication and authorization.

- Handling user input and managing dynamic content.

As you progress, consider adding features like search functionality, pagination, and complex CRUD operations. This will deepen your understanding of how to handle dynamic content and work with more advanced MySQL queries.

## Collaborate with Others

Collaborating on open-source projects or contributing to development teams can expose you to different coding styles, frameworks, and practices. Open-source platforms like **GitHub** are great places to find interesting projects where you can contribute and learn from more experienced developers.

## Seek Feedback and Iterate

Don't be afraid to ask for feedback from others. Sharing your work with other developers or mentors and incorporating their feedback will help you identify areas for improvement. Iterating on your projects and revising your code will refine your skills over time.

---

# Building and Growing Real-World Projects

Real-world projects help you hone your skills and expand your portfolio. The more projects you build, the better you'll understand the challenges faced by developers and how to solve them effectively.

## How to Start a Side Project

Starting a side project is a fantastic way to apply what you've learned while pursuing something you're passionate about. Here's how to get started:

1. **Choose a Project Idea**: Think of a problem you'd like to solve or a service you can provide. It could be something as simple as a **task manager** or as complex as an **online learning platform**.

2. **Plan the Project**: Break the project into smaller, manageable tasks. Create a rough roadmap of how you will approach the development process, starting with the most important features.

3. **Build Iteratively**: Don't try to build everything at once. Start with the basic functionality and then gradually add more features as you improve your skills.

4. **Test and Improve**: Always test your code. Address any bugs and performance issues before moving forward. Use **unit tests** to ensure that individual components are working correctly.

**Keep Improving Your Skills**

As you continue to build side projects, keep pushing yourself by tackling more challenging features, trying new frameworks, or learning about advanced topics like **API development**, **web security**, or **cloud computing**. Over time, you'll become more proficient and be able to take on larger, more complex projects.

---

Your journey of learning PHP, MySQL, and web development has only just begun. By following the advice and resources laid out in this book, you are well-equipped to continue mastering the art of web development. The key to success is consistent practice, continuous learning, and a willingness to push your limits. Keep building, experimenting, and learning from real-world projects, and you will grow into a skilled, confident developer ready to tackle any web development challenge.

Remember, web development is a journey, not a destination. Embrace every challenge, and don't be afraid to make mistakes—each one is an opportunity to learn and improve.

# Appendix: Glossary of Terms and Resources for Further Learning

This appendix serves as a helpful reference guide to reinforce key concepts and terms used throughout the book, as well as to provide resources for continued learning. As you continue to grow as a PHP and MySQL developer, having a strong understanding of terminology and a list of resources will make it easier to navigate the vast world of web development.

## Glossary of Terms

### 1. PHP (Hypertext Preprocessor)

PHP is a server-side scripting language primarily used for creating dynamic and interactive websites. It is open-source and runs on a web server, processing user requests and interacting with databases, such as MySQL, to deliver dynamic content.

### 2. MySQL

MySQL is an open-source relational database management system (RDBMS) that uses Structured Query Language (SQL) to manage databases. It stores data in tables and allows for efficient querying, manipulation, and retrieval of data.

### 3. Server-Side Programming

Server-side programming refers to code that runs on a web server rather than on a user's device (client-side). This code is responsible for handling requests, interacting with databases, and generating dynamic content that is sent to the user's browser.

### 4. Client-Side Programming

Client-side programming runs in the user's web browser and is responsible for handling interactions on the page, such as animations, form validation, and displaying dynamic content without involving the server.

### 5. SQL (Structured Query Language)

SQL is the standard programming language used to interact with relational databases. It is used for tasks like creating and modifying databases, inserting, updating, and deleting records, and querying data using statements like SELECT, INSERT, UPDATE, and DELETE.

### 6. Relational Database

A relational database is a type of database that stores data in tables that are linked to one another using relationships. Data is organized into rows and columns, and SQL is used to retrieve and manipulate the data stored in these tables.

### 7. CRUD Operations

CRUD stands for Create, Read, Update, and Delete. These are the basic operations that you can perform on database records. These operations form the backbone of many dynamic web applications, such as managing blog posts, users, and products.

## 8. MySQLi (MySQL Improved)

MySQLi is a PHP extension that allows developers to interact with MySQL databases. It offers enhanced functionality compared to the older mysql extension, such as prepared statements, better error handling, and support for multiple queries.

## 9. PDO (PHP Data Objects)

PDO is a database access library in PHP that provides a uniform interface for interacting with different database management systems, including MySQL, PostgreSQL, SQLite, and others. It is known for its support for prepared statements and its ability to prevent SQL injection.

## 10. Form Handling

Form handling in PHP involves creating forms that collect user input, validate the input, and process it for storage or use within a web application. Common actions include user registration, login, and contact forms.

## 11. Sessions

Sessions in PHP allow you to store user-specific data temporarily across multiple pages during a user's visit to a website. This is typically used for user authentication and to maintain user-specific preferences or settings.

## 12. Cookies

Cookies are small pieces of data stored on the client's browser, often used to remember a user's preferences, authentication information, or session state. Cookies can be persistent or temporary, depending on the needs of the website.

## 13. SQL Injection

SQL injection is a security vulnerability that allows attackers to manipulate SQL queries by injecting malicious code into input fields. To protect against SQL injection, it is essential to use parameterized queries or prepared statements.

## 14. XSS (Cross-Site Scripting)

XSS is a security vulnerability where attackers inject malicious scripts into webpages viewed by other users. These scripts can steal data, hijack user sessions, or perform other malicious actions. Preventing XSS involves properly sanitizing user input and escaping output.

## 15. CSRF (Cross-Site Request Forgery)

CSRF is a type of attack where an attacker tricks a user into making an unwanted request to a website, typically to perform an action that the user did not intend (such as changing a password). CSRF protection involves using tokens to verify that a request came from the intended user.

## 16. MVC (Model-View-Controller)

MVC is a design pattern used to separate an application's logic into three interconnected components:

- **Model**: Represents the data and business logic.

- **View**: Handles the presentation and user interface.

- **Controller**: Manages the flow of data between the Model and View, receiving user input and updating the model accordingly.

## 17. OOP (Object-Oriented Programming)

OOP is a programming paradigm based on the concept of "objects," which are instances of classes. Objects contain properties (data) and methods (functions) that define their behavior. OOP promotes reusable, maintainable, and scalable code.

## 18. SQL Join

A SQL join is an operation that combines rows from two or more tables based on a related column, often the primary key or foreign key. Common types of joins are **INNER JOIN**, **LEFT JOIN**, and **RIGHT JOIN**.

## 19. Prepared Statements

Prepared statements are a feature of both MySQLi and PDO that allow developers to write SQL queries where the query structure is defined beforehand, and the data is bound later. This enhances security and prevents SQL injection.

## 20. Eloquent ORM

Eloquent is an Object-Relational Mapping (ORM) tool provided by Laravel that simplifies database operations by representing database tables as classes. It enables you to interact with the database using PHP objects instead of raw SQL queries.

# Resources for Further Learning

As the web development landscape evolves, continuous learning is essential to staying up-to-date with the latest tools, best practices, and technologies. Here are some recommended resources to continue your journey into PHP, MySQL, and web development in general.

**Books**

1. **"PHP and MySQL Web Development" by Luke Welling and Laura Thomson** This book is a comprehensive guide for anyone looking to master PHP and MySQL. It covers a wide range of topics, from basic web programming to advanced database design and optimization.

2. **"Modern PHP: New Features and Good Practices" by Josh Lockhart** This book explores new features in PHP, such as namespaces, closures, and dependency injection, along with best practices for writing clean, maintainable code.

3. **"Learning SQL" by Alan Beaulieu** A beginner-friendly book that covers the basics of SQL, with a focus on practical examples and real-world applications. It's a great starting point for those looking to learn database design and management.

4. **"Laravel Up & Running" by Matt Stauffer** For those interested in learning the Laravel PHP framework, this book offers an excellent introduction to the framework's features, including routing, database operations, and authentication.

**Websites and Online Courses**

1. **PHP Manual** (https://www.php.net/manual/en/)
   The official PHP manual is an essential resource for learning PHP's functions, syntax, and libraries. It is regularly updated and provides detailed examples and documentation.

2. **MySQL Documentation** (https://dev.mysql.com/doc/) The MySQL documentation is the go-to resource for understanding how to use MySQL's features, perform database optimization, and write advanced queries.

3. **Laracasts** (https://laracasts.com) Known as the "Netflix for developers," Laracasts offers video tutorials focused on PHP and Laravel. It's an excellent resource for learning modern PHP development practices.

4. **Codecademy** (https://www.codecademy.com) Codecademy offers interactive courses on PHP, MySQL, and web development. The hands-on approach makes it an excellent resource for beginners.

5. **Udemy** (https://www.udemy.com) Udemy offers a range of courses on PHP, MySQL, web development, and specific frameworks like Laravel and Symfony. Courses range from beginner to advanced levels, and many are taught by industry experts.

6. **Stack Overflow** (https://stackoverflow.com) Stack Overflow is an essential community for web developers. It's an excellent resource for

troubleshooting specific issues and learning from other developers.

## Communities and Forums

1.  **PHP Manual Community** (https://www.php.net/community) The PHP manual community forum is a great place to discuss PHP-related issues with other developers and the PHP community.

2.  **r/PHP** on Reddit (https://www.reddit.com/r/PHP/) A subreddit for PHP developers, where you can share resources, ask questions, and discuss best practices.

3.  **Laravel Community** (https://laravel.io) The Laravel community forum offers a space for developers to share insights, ask questions, and collaborate on projects using the Laravel PHP framework.

4.  **GitHub** (https://github.com) GitHub is an excellent platform for exploring open-source PHP projects, collaborating on development, and contributing to existing repositories.

## Tools and Libraries

1.  **Xdebug** (https://xdebug.org) Xdebug is a debugging tool for PHP that allows you to step through code, inspect variables, and troubleshoot errors.

2.  **Composer** (https://getcomposer.org) Composer is a dependency management tool for PHP, used to

manage libraries and packages in your projects. It helps automate updates and keeps libraries up to date.

3. **PHPStan** (https://phpstan.org) PHPStan is a static analysis tool for PHP that helps catch bugs before they occur by analyzing your code for potential errors.

---

## Conclusion

Building dynamic websites with PHP and MySQL is a rewarding experience that offers countless opportunities to expand your skills. This glossary provides the foundational terms and concepts needed to better understand PHP and MySQL, and the resources listed here will help guide your continued learning. With dedication and practice, you can continue mastering these technologies and stay ahead of the curve in the ever-evolving world of web development.

Good luck, and enjoy the journey!

www.ingramcontent.com/pod-product-compliance
Lightning Source LLC
Chambersburg PA
CBHW070942050326
40689CB00014B/3314